Informing the legislative debate since 1914 _____

Climate Change and Existing Law: A Survey of Legal Issues Past, Present, and Future

Robert Meltz
Legislative Attorney

August 20, 2014

Congressional Research Service

7-5700

www.crs.gov

R42613

Summary

This report surveys *existing* law for legal issues that have arisen, or may arise in the future, on account of climate change and government responses thereto.

At the threshold of many climate-change-related lawsuits are two barriers—whether the plaintiff has standing to sue and whether the claim being made presents a political question. Both barriers have forced courts to apply amorphous standards in a new and complex context.

Efforts to mitigate climate change—i.e., reduce greenhouse gas (GHG) emissions—have spawned a host of legal issues. The Supreme Court resolved a big one in 2007: the Clean Air Act (CAA), it said, authorizes EPA to regulate GHG emissions. Most of EPA's subsequent efforts to carry out that authority have been sustained by the D.C. Circuit. In 2014, however, the Supreme Court held that EPA's regulation of GHG emissions from motor vehicles does not categorically bring GHG emissions from power plants and factories under the permitting sections of the Act. EPA's alternative track for regulating GHG emissions from such "stationary sources," standards of performance for new and existing sources, also raises issues. Still other mitigation issues are (1) the role of the Endangered Species Act in addressing climate change; (2) how climate change must be considered under the National Environmental Policy Act; (3) questions raised by carbon capture and sequestration; and (4) constitutional constraints on state actions to control GHG emissions.

Liability for harms allegedly caused by climate change has raised another crop of legal issues. The Supreme Court has held that the CAA bars federal judges from imposing their own limits on GHG emissions from power plants, suggesting that common law remedies will play little role in addressing climate change. Questions of insurance policy coverage are also likely to be litigated. Finally, the applicability of international law principles to climate change has yet to be resolved.

Water shortages thought to be induced by climate change likely will lead to litigation over the nature of water rights. Shortages have already prompted several lawsuits over whether cutbacks in water delivered from federal projects effect Fifth Amendment takings or breaches of contract.

Sea level rise and extreme precipitation linked to climate change raise questions as to (1) the effect of sea level rise on the beachfront owner's property line; (2) whether public beach access easements migrate with the landward movement of beaches; (3) design and operation of federal levees; and (4) government failure to take preventive measures against climate change harms.

Other adaptation responses to climate change raising legal issues, often property-rights related, are beach armoring (seawalls, bulkheads, etc.), beach renourishment, and "managed retreat" measures. Retreat measures seek to move existing development away from areas likely to be affected by floods and sea level rise, and to discourage new development there.

Natural disasters to which climate change contributes may prompt questions as to whether response actions taken in an emergency are subject to relaxed requirements and, similarly, as to the rebuilding of structures destroyed by such disasters just as they were before.

Finally, immigration and refugee law appear not to cover persons forced to relocate because of climate change impacts such as drought or sea level rise.

Contents

Contacts

This report surveys *existing* law for legal issues that have arisen, or may arise in the future, on account of climate change and government responses thereto. The reader interested in proposals for *new* laws to deal with climate change is referred to other works.[1] Of course, while this report covers many of the major legal issues that have emerged or may do so, the endless ramifications of climate change preclude any claim to exhaustiveness.

The report takes as its point of departure the current scientific consensus that climate change is occurring and, to the degree it continues, will cause sea level rise and extreme weather events.[2] Inclusion of some legal issues was based further on the predominant scientific view that human activities are contributing to climate change.[3]

Discussion of several topics in this report may have to be substantially modified or deleted if Congress enacts comprehensive climate change legislation, though prospects for Congress doing so now seem small. Congressional legislation might alter or displace the role of certain existing statutes, the Clean Air Act and the Endangered Species Act being prime candidates, for addressing climate change, or end the already limited availability of common law claims for that purpose.

I. Threshold Barriers to Litigation

Federal courts have evolved a variety of gatekeeper doctrines to ensure that only certain plaintiffs and certain types of claims can invoke their jurisdiction. Two of these doctrines, standing and political question, have posed daunting barriers for plaintiffs in climate change cases.

Standing doctrine. This principle flows from Article III of the Constitution, which limits the jurisdiction of courts created under that article (such as federal district courts) to "cases" or "controversies." These words are construed to require a person who sues in an Article III court to show (1) "injury in fact" (existing or imminent), (2) "causation" (a traceable connection between the injury in fact and defendant's conduct), and (3) "redressability" (plaintiff's injury is likely to be remedied by the relief plaintiff seeks).[4] A plaintiff not satisfying any of these elements is said to lack standing; his or her suit will be dismissed.

It should be apparent that a plaintiff complaining of injury from climate change may be thwarted by any of the three standing requirements. For example, how does such a plaintiff show the second element, causation? How does he show, say, that a drought that destroyed his crops was caused by climate change—indeed, by climate change to which the defendant's greenhouse gas

---

[1] *See, e.g.*, Michael B. Gerrard (ed.), GLOBAL CLIMATE CHANGE AND U.S. LAW (American Bar Ass'n 2007); Tom Mounteer (ed.), CLIMATE CHANGE DESKBOOK (Envtl. Law Inst. 2009); CRS Report R40556, *Market-Based Greenhouse Gas Control: Selected Proposals in the 111th Congress*, by Larry Parker, Brent D. Yacobucci, and Jonathan L. Ramseur.

[2] National Research Council, ADVANCING THE SCIENCE OF CLIMATE CHANGE 2 (2010). *See generally* CRS Report RL33849, *Climate Change: Science and Policy Implications*, by Jane A. Leggett.

[3] National Research Council, *supra* note 2, at 2.

[4] *See, e.g.*, Lujan v. Defenders of Wildlife, 504 U.S. 555, 560 (1992). When it is an organization that sues on behalf of its members, rather than an individual, the standing requirements are (1) the members (or some of them) must have standing to sue in their own right; (2) the interests the organization seeks to protect in the suit are germane to the organization's purpose; and (3) neither the claim asserted nor the relief requested requires the participation of individual members in the lawsuit. Hunt v. Washington State Apple Advertising Comm'n, 432 U.S. 333, 343 (1977).

(GHG) emissions contributed?[5] To be sure, in two climate change decisions, *Massachusetts v. EPA* in the Supreme Court[6] and *American Elec. Power Co. v. Connecticut* in the Second Circuit,[7] Article III standing was found—but specifically for *state* plaintiffs.[8] *Massachusetts* asserted that states are entitled to "special solicitude" when seeking to establish standing,[9] and both decisions noted the sovereign status of states as *parens patriae* (literally, father of the country).[10] Case law since these decisions, however, has rejected their extension to private plaintiffs, who have often encountered difficulty establishing standing in climate change cases.[11] Courts have not relaxed the traditional standing law requirements discerned in Article III just because climate change is involved. True, such plaintiffs may seek to avoid Article III standing issues by attempting to establish standing in state courts. But if, as is likely, the lawsuit takes aim at GHG emissions from out-of-state sources, the defendants are likely to remove the case to federal court under federal question or diversity jurisdiction. Thus the question of Article III standing likely will need to be faced.

A specialized issue is whether Indian tribes, by virtue of their inherent sovereignty, should also be able to establish standing through *parens patriae* status.[12] The argument for tribal *parens patriae* standing was rejected by the district court in *Native Village of Kivalina v. ExxonMobil Corp.*, a case in which an Alaskan native village seeks damages for coastal erosion allegedly caused by climate change to which the defendants' GHG emissions assertedly contribute.[13]

---

[5] *See, e.g.*, Native Village of Kivalina v. ExxonMobil Corp., 663 F. Supp. 2d 863, 880 (N.D. Cal. 2009) ("there is no realistic possibility of tracing any particular alleged effect of global warming to any particular emissions by any specific person ..."), *affirmed on other grounds*, 696 F.3d 849 (9th Cir. 2012), *cert. denied*, 133 S. Ct. 2390 (2013); Washington Envtl. Council v. Bellon, 732 F.3d 1131, 1143 (9th Cir. 2013) ("Attempting to establish a causal nexus in this case [seeking to force state agencies to limit GHG emissions from oil refineries in state] may be a particularly challenging task.... [T]here is limited scientific capability in assessing, detecting, or measuring the relationship between a certain GHG emission source and localized climate impacts in a given region.").

[6] 549 U.S. 497 (2007).

[7] 582 F.3d 309 (2d Cir. 2009), *reversed on other grounds*, 131 S. Ct. 2527 (2011) (affirming the Second Circuit's finding of standing by equally divided vote).

[8] *See generally* Kirsten Engle, *State Standing in Climate Change Lawsuits*, 26 J. Land Use & Envtl. L. 217 (2011).

[9] 549 U.S. at 520.

[10] *Massachusetts*, 549 U.S. at 518-520; Connecticut v. American Elec. Power Co., 582 F.3d 309, 338-339 (2d Cir. 2009), *reversed on other grounds*, 131 S. Ct. 2527 (2011). That is, Article III is satisfied when a state brings suit as *parens patriae* on behalf of its citizens. *Massachusetts*, 549 U.S. at 519-521.

Parens patriae doctrine allows a state to sue in its sovereign capacity to protect its citizenry, rather than being limited, as Article III would normally require, to asserting traditional particularized injuries to state interests. The modern origins of the doctrine lie in two century-old nuisance cases brought by states in federal court alleging interstate pollution: *Missouri v. Illinois*, 180 U.S. 208 (1901), and *Georgia v. Tennessee Copper Co.*, 206 U.S. 230 (1907). In both cases, state standing was found. The current test for *parens patriae* standing is found in *Snapp & Son, Inc. v. Puerto Rico*, 458 U.S. 592 (1982), though there is some question whether traditional Article III standing requirements have to be met as well by the citizens of the state asserting *parens patriae* standing. *See generally*, Sara Zdeb, *From* Georgia v. Tennessee Copper *to* Massachusetts v. EPA; *Parens Patriae Standing for State Global Warming Plaintiffs*, 96 Geo. L. J. 1059 (2008).

[11] *See, e.g.*, Comer v. Murphy Oil USA, Inc., 839 F. Supp. 2d 849 (S.D. Miss. 2012) (finding of Article III standing for state sovereign in *Massachusetts v. EPA* does not support standing for private plaintiffs here), *affirmed on other grounds*, 718 F.3d 460 (5th Cir. 2013); Native Village of Kivalina v. ExxonMobil Corp., 663 F. Supp. 2d 863, 882 (N.D. Cal. 2009) (same), *affirmed on other grounds*, 696 F.3d 849 (9th Cir. 2012), *cert. denied*, 133 S. Ct. 2390 (2013); Washington Envtl. Council v. Bellon, 732 F.3d 1131, 1145 (9th Cir. 2013) (same).

[12] *See generally* Elizabeth Ann Kronk, *Effective Access to Justice: Applying the Parens Patriae Standing Doctrine to Climate Change-Related Claims Brought by Native Nations*, 32 Pub. Land & Res. L. Rev. 1 (2011).

[13] 663 F. Supp. 2d at 882.

Standing issues have arisen in most of the many cases challenging the adequacy of agencies' discussion of climate change in environmental impact statements, where the partially relaxed requirements for standing based on procedural injury apply.[14]

Political question doctrine. While standing asks whether there is a proper *plaintiff* before the court, political question doctrine asks whether there is a justiciable *claim*. The doctrine seeks to restrain courts from inappropriate interference in the business of the other branches of government—often because resolving the issue necessarily involves policy determinations. Six factors indicating a non-justiciable political question (any one of which may be dispositive) were famously stated by the Supreme Court in *Baker v. Carr* in 1962.[15] Of these, the first three have played a role in the climate-change nuisance cases: "a textually demonstrable constitutional commitment of the issue to a coordinate political department; or a lack of judicially discoverable and manageable standards for resolving it; or the impossibility of deciding [the issue] without an initial policy determination of a kind clearly for nonjudicial discretion.... "

Baker made clear it was setting a high threshold for nonjusticiability; since it was decided a half-century ago, the Court has found few issues to present political questions. But the doctrine has been ubiquitous in the nuisance-based climate change litigation with more courts rejecting such claims on that ground than not.[16]

Addendum. At this point, the reader is referred to Section III.A., "A. Liability After American Electric Power Co., Inc. v. Connecticut," which discusses yet another litigation barrier: federal displacement of common-law-based climate change claims by the Clean Air Act. This barrier, announced by the Supreme Court in 2011, now makes it unnecessary for courts to reach the standing and political question issues in the case, allowing them to avoid the abstruse questions raised by those defenses.[17]

---

[14] *See, e.g.,* WildEarth Guardians v. Jewell, 738 F.3d 298 (D.C. Cir. 2013) (harm to group's members from local pollution caused by federal leasing of coal lands was sufficient injury in fact to allow challenge to *all* of alleged deficiencies in environmental impact statement on proposed lease, including those related to climate change).

[15] 369 U.S. 186, 216 (1962).

[16] Two decisions rejecting common-law claims based on climate-change harms, on political question grounds, are *Native Village of Kivalina*, 63 F. Supp. 2d at 871-877, and *Comer*, 839 F. Supp. 2d at 862-865. Both decisions based their rejection of the claims on the second and third *Baker* factors noted in the text. Declining to accept a political question defense for such claims is *American Electric Power v. Connecticut*, 582 F.3d 309, 323-332 (2d Cir. 2009), *reversed on other grounds*, 131 S. Ct. 2527 (2011). In contrast with these differing views in the common law realm, no difference of judicial opinion exists when a climate change claim is based on failure to satisfy requirements in a *statute*, such as the Clean Air Act. There, the claim avoids the absence of clear standards in the common law cases and dismissal on political question grounds is deemed inappropriate. *See, e.g., Massachusetts*, 549 U.S. at 516 (proper construction of a congressional statute, here the Clean Air Act, is a question "eminently suitable to resolution in a federal court").

[17] This is exactly what the Ninth Circuit did in its *Kivalina* affirmance in 2012, *supra* note 11. Following the district court's rejection of the common-law nuisance claim on standing and political question grounds, the circuit court rejected the claim solely on the basis of the CAA displacement argument announced by the Supreme Court since the district court ruled.

II. Mitigation—Reducing GHG Emissions

Proactive responses to climate change are usually grouped under one of two headings: mitigation and adaptation. This section treats some of the legal issues raised by mitigation. Sections IV and V compile some of the legal issues associated with adaptation.

A. *Massachusetts v. EPA* and GHG Rules Under the Clean Air Act So Far

In 2007, the Supreme Court answered a key Clean Air Act (CAA) question. The act, it found in *Massachusetts v. EPA*,[18] gives EPA authority to regulate GHG emissions. Such authority is granted, said the Court, because the CAA term "air pollutant" is defined sufficiently broadly in the act to include GHGs. Moreover, the Court added, the CAA forecloses an EPA decision not to regulate GHGs or any other air pollutant simply because the administration in power may have policy qualms—for example, due to a preference for non-regulatory approaches. In light of these determinations, the Court instructed EPA to reconsider its 2003 denial of a petition asking it to regulate GHG emissions from new motor vehicles, a denial EPA had based on the Court-rejected reasons.[19]

Following the *Massachusetts* decision, EPA set about the task of adapting the CAA to address climate change. In doing so, the agency confronted a statute more comfortably suited to regional air pollution problems, the opposite of climate change with its global nature. Four early EPA actions in that effort are:

- **The "timing rule."** 75 *Federal Register* 17004 (2010). This "rule," actually an EPA memorandum, concluded that PSD requirements for stationary sources of GHGs would take effect on January 2, 2011, when the "tailpipe rule" (below) took effect.

- **The "endangerment finding."** 74 *Federal Register* 66496 (2009). In this rule, EPA determined that GHG emissions from new motor vehicles "cause, or contribute to, air pollution which may reasonably be anticipated to endanger public health or welfare," per CAA section 202(a)(1). The finding has no effect in itself; its importance is that it triggers a duty under CAA section 202(a) for EPA to promulgate emission standards for new motor vehicles—see immediately below.

- **The "tailpipe rule."** 75 *Federal Register* 25323 (2010). In this rule, EPA and the National Highway Traffic Safety Administration set, respectively, GHG emission standards and fuel economy standards for 2012-2016 model year light-duty vehicles.

- **The "tailoring rule."** 75 *Federal Register* 31514 (2010). This rule aimed to relieve the overwhelming permitting burdens that EPA asserted would, in the absence of the rule, fall on "prevention of significant deterioration" (PSD) and

---

[18] 549 U.S. 497 (2007).

[19] 68 Fed. Reg. 52,922 (2003).

Title V permitting authorities beginning January 2, 2011, when EPA's tailpipe rule took effect. When that happened, the PSD part of the CAA requires that PSD permits be issued, and "best available control technology" (BACT) applied, for every new major emitting facility (and major modification) in the PSD area that emits more than either 100 or 250 tons of pollutant annually, depending on the source. This is a huge number of sources, so the tailoring rule set much higher tonnage thresholds, gradually diminishing, EPA hoped, in following years.

In 2012, the D.C. Circuit upheld all these EPA actions.[20] The Supreme Court granted certiorari, but limited to one narrow question: "[w]hether EPA permissibly determined that its regulation of greenhouse gas emissions from new motor vehicles triggered permitting requirements under the [CAA] for stationary sources that emit greenhouse gases." The "permitting requirements ... for stationary sources" to which the Court referred are those under the PSD new source review and Title V operating permit portions of the CAA.

In 2014, the Supreme Court handed down *Utility Air Regulatory Group v. EPA (UARG),*[21] answering no to the above question—that is, EPA's regulation of vehicle GHG emissions does *not* give EPA unqualified authority to apply PSD new source permitting and Title V operating permits to stationary source GHG emissions. As the Court explained, just because the CAA phrase "air pollutant" generally extends to GHGs, as it held in *Massachusetts*, does not mean the phrase includes GHGs every place in the Act it is used, such as in the PSD and Title V sections.[22] In these permit programs, extending "air pollutant" to GHG emissions creates a staggering administrative workload owing to the low emission thresholds that trigger those programs and the huge number of sources that satisfy those thresholds for CO_2, the primary GHG. This unwieldy result argued strongly, in the Court's view, against a GHG-inclusive reading of the two permit programs.[23] Nor did the Court allow EPA, through its "Tailoring Rule" (above), to phase in the low statutory emission thresholds in an effort to ease the daunting permit-issuing workload, since the CAA states the thresholds in absolute numerical terms.[24]

On the other hand, the Court allowed that when PSD new source permitting is required because a new (or modified) source emits a "conventional" pollutant in threshold quantities, then EPA also may impose PSD new-source permitting on GHG emissions from that source.[25] According to the United States, such "anyway" sources, so called because they are covered independently of their CO_2 emissions, account for roughly 83% of American stationary source GHG emissions. For this reason, the Court's decision may be regarded as a qualified win for EPA, even though its Tailoring Rule was invalidated.

The narrowness of the question that the Court answered in *UARG* is significant, since it leaves intact the D.C. Circuit's approval of EPA's endangerment finding for GHG emissions from new motor vehicles, not to mention the *Massachusetts v. EPA* holding. Nor did *UARG* directly touch

---

[20] Coalition for Responsible Regulation, Inc. v. EPA, 684 F.3d 102 (D.C. Cir. 2012).

[21] 134 S. Ct. 2427 (2014).

[22] *Id.* at 2439-2432.

[23] *Id.* at 2442-2444.

[24] *Id.* at 2444-2446.

[25] *Id.* at 2444-2449.

on the validity of EPA's current use of CAA section 111 in its effort to control GHG emissions from new and existing fossil-fuel-fired power plants.[26]

B. Future GHG Rules Under the Clean Air Act

Mentions of climate change in President Obama's second inaugural address and his 2013 and 2014 State of the Union speeches sought to reactivate the climate change debate on Capitol Hill. Particularly relevant to this section of the report is the President's 2013 State of the Union statement that if Congress does not act on climate change "soon," he will "direct [his] cabinet to come up with executive actions we can take.... " The President's Climate Action Plan, accompanied by a directive to EPA,[27] underscored in June, 2013 what was already clear from his State of the Union remark: that many of these "executive actions" will be under the CAA. This raises among other issues the following.

1. Endangerment Findings

With EPA's endangerment finding for new motor vehicle GHG emissions having survived judicial challenge, a question arises: Does that finding, made under CAA section 202, legally compel the agency to make endangerment findings for GHG emissions under other sections of the act that use similar endangerment language for other types of emission sources? Such subsequent endangerment findings would require, or at least authorize, EPA to regulate GHG emissions under those sections.

The CAA section most likely to require EPA regulatory action after the section 202 endangerment finding is section 111. Section 111 requires EPA to set performance standards for those categories of new stationary sources of emissions that "cause, or contribute significantly to, air pollution which may reasonably be anticipated to endanger public health or welfare."[28] As Section II.B.3 below notes, this issue is now moot: in January 2014, EPA made an endangerment finding and proposed new source performance standards for GHG emissions from fossil fuel-fired power plants, pursuant to litigation settlements and the President's 2013 directive.[29]

---

[26] CAA section 111(b) authorizes EPA to set "new source performance standards," emission standards for new stationary sources. CAA section 111(d) authorizes the agency to set emission standards for existing stationary sources that would be covered had they been new, among other preconditions.

[27] Presidential Memorandum: Power Sector Carbon Pollution Standards, 78 Fed. Reg. 39,535 (July 1, 2013) (announced June 25, 2013). *See generally* CRS Report R43127, *EPA Standards for Greenhouse Gas Emissions from Power Plants: Many Questions, Some Answers*, by James E. McCarthy.

[28] 42 U.S.C. § 7411(b)(1)(A).

[29] EPA's position is more nuanced than the text suggests. As with its endangerment finding for motor vehicles in 2009, the agency argues that a section 111 endangerment finding has two independent components: a determination that a pollutant or set of pollutants "may reasonably be anticipated to endanger public health or welfare" and a determination that the source category proposed to be regulated "cause[s] or contribute[s] significantly" to that pollution. EPA contends that it needs only a rational basis for these two determinations, and that such a rational basis exists for regulating GHG emissions from new fossil fuel-fired power plant regulation under section111. The first determination—that six "well-mixed" pollutants collectively, by causing climate change, endanger public health or welfare— has already been made, as part of the 2009 endangerment finding. The second determination—that fossil fuel-fired power plants contribute significantly to that air pollution— is evident, EPA asserts, from the fact that "electricity generating plants, as an industry, constitute, by a significant margin, the largest emitters [of GHGs] in the inventory." Importantly, the agency reads section 111(b)(1)(A) to not require separate determinations for each pollutant emitted by a source category, such as CO_2. In the event, the courts reject this reading, however, EPA proposes a (continued...)

Second, two other CAA provisions that might be triggered by the section 202 endangerment finding are section 108,[30] requiring national ambient air quality standards, and section 115,[31] which requires states to revise their implementation plans to prevent or eliminate the endangerment of public health or welfare in a foreign country. As to these sections, however, the arguable infeasibility of achieving the regulatory goals—even if GHG emissions in the United States are significantly reduced, atmospheric concentrations would decline little—may give EPA room to argue that regulatory action is not mandatory. Other endangerment-triggered sections of the CAA can be distinguished from section 202(a) by their explicit terms, and so likely would not be triggered by the 202(a) endangerment finding, or at least do not impose on EPA a *mandatory* duty to promulgate GHG emission limits even once an endangerment finding is made.

Since the 2007 decision in *Massachusetts v. EPA*, EPA has been petitioned to make endangerment findings under almost all the CAA sections just mentioned, but has finally ruled on none. This inaction raises the question of whether the agency can be compelled to act on these petitions after a sufficient number of years. The CAA allows citizen suits against EPA to compel agency action when such action is "unreasonably delayed," but only for agency actions that are "not discretionary." Thus courts will have to determine, as an initial matter, which of the endangerment-finding provisions in the CAA impose nondiscretionary duties on the agency.[32]

2. Cap-and-Trade Authority

Should EPA, per the previous section, make endangerment findings under CAA sections other than 202, the question has arisen whether those sections allow cap-and-trade or other flexible approaches to GHG emissions control.[33] Under cap and trade, emission allowances would be traded among sources, allowing the market to allocate the available total ("cap") of emissions.

The CAA sections often implicated in this debate are sections 111(d)[34] (existing stationary sources in categories for which a standard of performance has been promulgated for new sources), 115[35] (international air pollution), 211[36] (fuels), 213[37] (nonroad engines and vehicles),

---

(...continued)

separate "cause or contribute significantly" determination for CO_2 emitted by the fossil fuel-fired power plant category. 79 Fed. Reg. 1430, 1453 (2014).

EPA points out that in contrast with the absence in section 111 of any prerequisite that for EPA to issue a standard of performance, it must first determine that the particular pollutant causes or contributes significantly to air pollution that endangers public health or welfare, other CAA sections *do* require EPA to make both determinations for a particular pollutant to regulate under those sections. *Id.*

[30] 42 U.S.C. § 7408.

[31] 42 U.S.C. § 7415.

[32] For contrary decisions as to the endangerment finding provision in CAA section 231, which governs aircraft emissions, compare *Friends of the Earth v. EPA*, 2013 Westlaw 1226822 (D.D.C. March 27, 2013) (EPA duty to rule on endangerment under section 231 is discretionary, so no citizen suit lies) with *Center for Biological Diversity v. EPA*, 794 F. Supp. 2d 151 (D.D.C. 2011) (said duty is nondiscretionary, so citizen suit lies if there is unreasonable delay).

[33] *See, e.g.*, Nathan Richardson, *Playing Without Aces: Offsets and the Limits of Flexibility Under Clean Air Act Climate Policy*, 42 Envtl. L. 735 (2012).

[34] 42 U.S.C. § 7411(d).

[35] 42 U.S.C. § 7415.

[36] 42 U.S.C. § 7545.

[37] 42 U.S.C. § 7547.

---

and 231[38] (aircraft). None of these CAA sections, however, say anything explicit about cap and trade, either to authorize it or prohibit it. On the no-authority side, each section, to varying degrees, makes cap and trade an awkward fit.[39] Further, the CAA expressly authorizes cap and trade in two places: subtitle IV[40] addressing acid deposition and section 110(a)(2)(A)[41] setting out elements of state implementation plans for achieving national ambient air quality standards. These explicit mentions of cap and trade give rise to the negative implication that where Congress has not clearly indicated authority for cap and trade, such authority is not granted. Still, the question of CAA authority for GHG cap-and-trade programs must be deemed an open one.

The cap-and-trade issue is likely to receive its first litigation test when EPA finalizes its proposed rule for GHG emissions from existing fossil fuel-fired power plants,[42] expected in June, 2015. EPA has maintained consistently that CAA section 111(d), the authority for the proposed rule, is broad enough to allow compliance through cap and trade.[43]

3. Other Section 111 Issues

Proposed EPA regulations limiting GHG emissions from fossil-fuel power plants have cast an intense spotlight on ambiguities in two subsections of CAA section 111. The first-proposed regulations, published January 2014,[44] cover *new* plants and are governed by subsection (b); the second-proposed regulations, published June 2014, deal with *existing* plants and are governed by subsection (d).[45] It is a near certainty that the issues noted below, plus the cap-and-trade issue already mentioned, will be litigated once final rules under 111(b) and 111(d) are issued.

Both 111(b) and 111(d) call for "standards of performance," applicable to new and existing stationary sources, respectively. Section 111(a), in turn, defines "standard of performance" as an emission standard that "reflects the degree of emission reduction *achievable* through ... the *best system of emission reduction* which (*taking into account* ... cost ...) the [EPA] Administrator determines has been *adequately demonstrated*."[46] Each of the four italicized phrases raises issues.

As regards the proposed section 111(b) rule for new power plants, most attention targets the phrase "adequately demonstrated." The reason is plain: the proposed rule cannot be satisfied, by the agency's admission, without partial reliance on carbon capture and sequestration (CCS), a technology whose viability in connection with power generation is vigorously debated. So is CCS "adequately demonstrated" for power plants? Case law on the meaning of "adequately demonstrated" is ample, holding that the phrase does not necessarily imply that any existing

---

[38] 42 U.S.C. § 7571.

[39] EPA has adopted a NOx averaging, trading, and banking program for heavy-duty vehicles under CAA section 202. 40 C.F.R. § 86.1817-05.

[40] 42 U.S.C. § 7651 et seq.

[41] 42 U.S.C. § 7410(a)(2)(A).

[42] *Carbon Pollution Emission Guidelines for Existing Stationary Sources: Electric Utility Generating Units*, 79 Fed. Reg. 34830 (2014).

[43] *See, e.g., id. at* 34927 and 40 C.F.R. § 60.21(f). Several commentators also conclude that section 111(d) embraces cap and trade. *See, e.g.,* Gregory Wannier at al. (Resources for the Future), *Prevailing Academic View on Compliance Flexibility Under Sec. 111 of the Clean Air Act*, Discussion Paper 11-29 (2011).

[44] 79 Fed. Reg. 1430 (January 8, 2014).

[45] *See* note 42 *supra*.

[46] 42 U.S.C. § 7411(a)(1).

source of the type proposed for a new source performance standard is able to meet the standard.[47] Rather, section 111 "looks toward what may fairly be projected for the regulated future, rather than the state of the art at present.... "[48] Such prognostication, however, may not be based on "mere speculation or conjecture ... ," though EPA may extrapolate from a technology's performance in other industries.[49]

The admitted reliance of EPA's proposed rule on CCS may also create an issue as to whether the proposed rule can be reconciled with the section 111(b)(5) ban on EPA's requiring any particular system of emission reduction to comply with a NSPS.[50]

Section 111(d) raises its own set of legal issues. That subsection mandates that states develop standards of performance for existing sources for which a NSPS has been established—but only for pollutants meeting certain conditions. One of these conditions raises a critical threshold issue for the proposed rule, asking whether EPA may regulate CO_2 emissions from existing power plants *at all*. The issue arises from the fact that in the 1990 amendments to the CAA, inconsistent House and Senate amendments to section 111(d) were passed, and not reconciled in conference. Under the House amendment, section 111(d) standards of performance are not authorized for air pollutants "emitted from a source category ... regulated under section 112," which covers hazardous air pollutants. Because fossil-fuel-fired power plants *are* a source category regulated under section 112, this argument concludes that section 111(d) does not allow EPA to restrict GHG emissions from existing such plants. The Senate amendment, by contrast, places off limits only *air pollutants* regulated under section 112. CO_2 *is not* an air pollutant regulated under section 112, so the Senate amendment is not an obstacle to the proposed 111(d) rule. In the upcoming litigation, EPA likely will argue that Congress could not have intended such a major carve-out from section 111(d)'s coverage without being more explicit, and that in light of the ambiguity created by the inconsistent amendments, the court should defer to EPA's effort to reconcile them.

Another section 111(d) issue turns on the degree of flexibility it allows. In EPA's view, "[s]ection 111(d) provides greater flexibility to EPA and states to design a program in consultation with [a] diverse range of stakeholders."[51] But does this flexibility extend beyond the traditional approach of imposing emission limits on individual power plants to embrace so-called "beyond the fenceline" approaches? The question of whether a cap-and-trade approach is authorized was noted earlier, but EPA's recently proposed section 111(d) rule goes much further. It bases its determination of the "best system of emission reduction" (see definition of "standard of performance" above) for each state on varying combinations of four "building blocks"—that is, four ways of reducing CO_2 emissions from existing power plants. Three of these four building buildings may be described as "beyond the fenceline"—building block two (substituting natural gas-fired generation for coal-fired generation); building block three (substituting low- or zero-carbon generation, such as nuclear power), and building block four (improvements in demand-side energy efficiency). Will the fact that CO_2 emissions differ from the pollutants that have been regulated in the past under section 111(d) dispose the court to allow EPA enough leeway for such approaches?

---

[47] *See, e.g.,* Portland Cement Ass'n v. Ruckelshaus, 486 F.3d 375, 391 (D.C. Cir. 1973).

[48] *Id.*

[49] Lignite Energy Council v. EPA, 198 F.3d 930, 934 (D.C. Cir. 1999).

[50] 42 U.S.C. § 7411(b)(5).

[51] Powerpoint presentation of Mr. Kevin Culligan, EPA Office of Air and Radiation, presented January 30, 2014 at seminar on GHG regulations for the power sector.

Finally, if a state fails to submit a "satisfactory" plan under section 111(d), EPA has authority to promulgate, and if necessary enforce, a plan (or portion of a plan) for the state.[52] Does that authority go so far as to allow EPA regulation of activities covered by building blocks three and four—activities that go beyond anything EPA is authorized to regulate elsewhere in the CAA, and that trench on the jurisdiction of other federal and state agencies?

C. Use of the Endangered Species Act to Restrict GHG Emissions[53]

Some cast the Endangered Species Act (ESA) as a tool aggressive environmental groups may use to thwart projects that produce GHGs. Under this view, plaintiffs would claim that a project's GHG emissions, by contributing to climate change that brings about adverse habitat change, are causing a "take" of protected species in violation of the ESA.[54] For example, a suit could claim that any project that contributes to warmer seas harms, hence "takes," certain listed coral species. However, no case law can be found on this legal argument, either accepting or rejecting it.

Instead of alleging takes of species, lawsuits connecting the ESA to climate change typically are based on how an agency considered climate change when making other determinations: listing a species;[55] designating critical habitat;[56] or issuing a Biological Opinion.[57] The ESA requires that the Fish & Wildlife Service (FWS) consider the effects on habitat, at least in part, for all of those determinations.[58] Accordingly, climate change evaluations long have been part of ESA decision-making, but only to the extent that the climate's effects on habitat are linked to a species.

Case law does not show that the ESA is used as an enforcement tool to make climate change arguments. In the handful of cases where ESA challenges were directed at federal projects related to power plants, only one involved climate change allegations, *Palm Beach County Environmental Coalition v. Florida*, and it was not clear whether those claims were premised on the ESA or on another legal basis.[59]

---

[52] CAA § 111(d)(2); 42 U.S.C. § 7411(d)(2).

[53] This section of the report was written by Kristina Alexander, Legislative Attorney, CRS American Law Division.

[54] Habitat change can constitute a "take" of listed species as follows. Under the ESA, "take" is defined as "to harass, harm, pursue, hunt, shoot, wound, kill, trap, capture, or collect, or to attempt to engage in any such conduct." 16 U.S.C. § 1532(19). "Harm" in this definition has been defined by the Fish & Wildlife Service to include "significant habitat modification or degradation where it actually kills or injures wildlife." 50 C.F.R. § 17.3.

[55] *See, e.g.*, Greater Yellowstone Coalition, Inc. v. Servheen, 665 F.3d 1015 (9th Cir. 2011); In re Polar Bear Endangered Species Act Listing, 794 F. Supp. 2d 65 (D.D.C. 2011); Center for Biological Diversity v. Lubchenco, 758 F. Supp. 2d 945 (N.D. Cal. 2010).

[56] *See, e.g.*, Conservancy of Southwest Florida v. U.S. Fish and Wildlife Service, 2011 Westlaw 1326805 (M.D. Fla. April 6, 2011); Alliance for Wild Rockies v. Lyder, 728 F. Supp. 2d 1126 (D. Mont. 2010).

[57] *See, e.g.*, Center for Biological Diversity v. Salazar, 804 F. Supp. 2d 987 (D. Ariz. 2011); South Yuba River Citizens League v. National Marine Fisheries Service, 723 F. Supp. 2d 1247 (E.D. Cal. 2010); and Pacific Coast Fed'n of Fishermen's Ass'ns v. Gutierrez, 606 F. Supp. 2d 1122 (E.D. Cal. 2008).

[58] *See* ESA § 4(a)(1)(A), 16 U.S.C. § 1533(a)(1)(A) (when making determination on whether to list a species, relevant wildlife agency must consider "the present or threatened destruction, modification, or curtailment of its habitat or range"); ESA § 4(b)(2), 16 U.S.C. § 1533(b)(2) (requiring relevant wildlife agency to designate critical habitat); and ESA § 7(a)(2), 16 U.S.C. § 1536(a)(2) (requiring all agencies to consult with relevant wildlife agency to determine whether their actions would "result in the destruction or adverse modification of habitat of such species which is determined ... to be critical").

[59] Palm Beach County Environmental Coalition v. Florida, 651 F. Supp. 2d 1328 (S.D. Fla. 2009). Plaintiffs also had alleged violations of the Clean Air Act, National Environmental Policy Act, and the Clean Water Act.

Despite the apparent lack of litigation premised on climate change *taking* species, some regulatory changes were made to limit lawsuits based on that cause of action. In 2008, FWS changed the regulations that dictated how a service considered impacts of federal projects on listed species.[60] Those regulations were effective only from January 15, 2008, to May 5, 2008, after Congress acted to halt them in P.L. 111-8.[61] During that period of regulatory change, definitions related to the effects of an agency action were modified to "reinforce the Services' current view that there is no requirement to consult on [greenhouse gas] emissions' contribution to global warming and its associated impacts on listed species."[62] Despite the revocation of those changes, it does not appear that the scope of effects has expanded, likely due to the fact that the regulations already limited review to those effects with a reasonable certainty to occur.[63]

Another regulatory change of the same time period is still in place. It restricts lawsuits claiming incidental takes of polar bears to instances where the agency action occurs in the state of Alaska.[64]

D. Consideration of Climate Change in Environmental Impact Statements

It is no longer in doubt that the National Environmental Policy Act (NEPA)[65] requires a federal agency to consider climate change impacts in environmental impact statements (EISs).[66] The obligation extends to both climate change impacts the agency's proposed project may contribute to, and those affecting the proposed project. The very first appearance of climate change in a reported court decision was in a NEPA case,[67] and the numerous NEPA/climate-change decisions since have never doubted that where sufficiently serious and causally connected to the project, climate change impacts should be discussed.[68] Draft guidance from the Council on Environmental Quality (CEQ)[69] and a recent CEQ letter[70] also make the point.

---

[60] 73 Fed. Reg. 76,272 (December 16, 2008) (effective January 15, 2009).

[61] 74 Fed. Reg. 20,421 (May 8, 2009) ("With this final rule, the Department of the Interior and the Department of Commerce amend regulations governing interagency cooperation under [the ESA]. In accordance with the statutory authority set forth in the 2009 Omnibus Appropriations Act (P.L. 111-8), this rule implements the regulations that were in effect immediately before the effective date of the regulation issued on December 16, 2008").

[62] 73 Fed. Reg. at 47872.

[63] 50 C.F.R. § 402.02.

[64] 50 C.F.R. § 17.40(q)(4). The polar bear was listed under the act primarily due to shrinking habitat caused by changing climate. 73 Fed. Reg. 28,212 (2008). The polar bear regulation prevents a lawsuit claiming that a power plant in any state other than Alaska harmed the polar bear by indirectly causing its ice floe habitat to diminish. The law that authorized revocation of the regulations discussed above, P.L. 111-8, also authorized revocation of the polar bear rule, but the Secretary of the Interior and the Secretary of Commerce did not act on that authority to revoke the rule.

[65] 42 U.S.C. §§ 4321-4370f.

[66] *See* NEPA § 102(2)(C); 42 U.S.C. § 4332(2)(C).

[67] City of Los Angeles v. National Highway Traffic Safety Admin., 912 F.2d 478 (D.C. Cir. 1990).

[68] *See, e.g.*, Center for Biological Diversity v. National Highway Traffic Safety Admin., 508 F.3d 508, 550 (9th Cir. 2007) ("The impact of greenhouse gas emissions is precisely the kind of cumulative impacts analysis that NEPA requires agencies to conduct."). There is now some support for use of the government's social cost of carbon protocol as part of an environmental impact statement's analysis of the climate-change-related costs of a proposed action. High Country Conservation Advocates v.U.S. Forest Service, 2014 WL 2922751 (D. Colo. June 27, 2014) (citing February, 2010 Technical Support Document of the Interagency Working Group on the Social Cost of Carbon).

[69] CEQ, Memorandum for Heads of Federal Departments and Agencies, *Draft NEPA Guidance on Consideration of the Effects of Climate Change and Greenhouse Gas Emissions* (February 18, 2010). As to a proposed project's possible contribution to climate change, the guidance states that "where a proposed Federal action that is analyzed in an (continued...)

Still, clear thresholds triggering EIS inclusion have yet to emerge from the court decisions. CEQ suggests in its draft guidance that when federal activity is subject to GHG emissions accounting requirements, such as CAA reporting requirements that apply to stationary sources that directly emit 25,000 metric tons or more of CO_2-equivalent GHG on an annual basis,[71] the agency should include this information in the NEPA documentation for consideration by decision makers and the public. CEQ expressly disclaims, however, that it intends 25,000 metric tons per year as the emission level that constitutes a "major federal action significantly affecting the quality of the human environment,"[72] NEPA's trigger for requiring an agency to prepare an EIS. Further ambiguity as to the threshold for including climate change effects in EISs stems from CEQ's requirement that EISs include "indirect effects" of the proposed federal action, not only direct ones, while defining indirect effects only loosely.[73]

Reportedly, "while most federal agencies now address climate change to some extent in the [EISs] they prepare, the specific impacts considered and the methodology used in these analyses vary widely."[74] This lack of uniformity has created pressure on CEQ to finalize its draft guidance, now over four years old, on consideration of climate change in NEPA environmental reviews.

In addition to the federal NEPA, many states have NEPA-like statutes for evaluating proposals of state agencies. The legal issues raised by climate change under these "little NEPAs" are beyond the scope of this report. An example is the former split in the lower California courts on whether projected *future* conditions—as in a climate-changed world—rather than current conditions can be used as the baseline for evaluating the environmental impacts of proposed state projects. The California Supreme Court recently held that an environmental impact report under the state's NEPA counterpart may omit the project's impacts on existing conditions and substitute a future baseline, if doing so is properly justified.[75]

(...continued)

[environmental assessment] or EIS would be anticipated to emit GHGs to the atmosphere in quantities that the agency finds may be meaningful, it is appropriate for the agency to quantify and disclose its estimate of the expected annual direct and indirect GHG emissions in the environmental documentation for the proposed action." *Id.* at 2. As to a proposed project's potential for being affected by future climate change, the guidance is equally unequivocal: "CEQ proposes that agencies should determine which climate change impacts warrant consideration in their [environmental assessments] and EISs because of their impact on the analysis of the environmental effects of a proposed agency action." *Id.* at 6.

[70] Letter from Michael Boots, Acting Chair, CEQ, to International Center for Technology Assessment et al., dated Aug. 7, 2014, responding to a petition for rulemaking and issuance of guidance to require inclusion of climate change analyses in NEPA documents. In denying the petition, the letter gives as one reason for CEQ not revising its existing NEPA regulations that "they already encompass consideration of climate effects ...." *Id.* at 2.

[71] 40 C.F.R. § 98.2.

[72] NEPA § 102(2)(C); 42 U.S.C. § 4332(2)(C).

[73] 40 C.F.R. § 1500.8(b). *See, e.g.,* Mid States Coalition for Progress v. Surface Transp. Bd., 345 F.3d 520 (8th Cir. 2003) (noting that EISs must include indirect effects of proposed federal actions, court holds that EIS on proposed rail line making it cheaper for coal to reach power plants must discuss effects of increased coal consumption).

[74] Jean Chemnick, *White House still hashing out how agencies should address climate in NEPA process,* Energy & Env't News, March 15, 2013.

[75] Neighbors for Smart Rail v. Exposition Metro Line Construction Auth., 2013 Westlaw 3970107 (Cal. August 5, 2013).

E. Carbon Capture and Sequestration[76]

While most proposals to mitigate climate change have focused on limiting GHG emissions at the smokestack or tailpipe, an option that has been discussed in recent years is carbon capture and sequestration (CCS). CCS is a process whereby CO_2 emissions would be "captured" at their source and then stored or "sequestered," rather than being released into the atmosphere. Frequently, this storage/sequestration would take place underground.

Large-scale CCS technology is still in the early stages of development. Therefore, there are a number of operational questions to be answered before we can fully understand all the legal issues that may arise. However, because the development of CCS technology could well depend in part upon the resolution of some of these legal issues, it is important to understand them as the CCS debate continues. Among the emerging legal issues associated with CCS technology are (1) who owns and controls the underground pore space where the CO_2 would be "sequestered" under many of the CCS facility concepts proposed, in particular is pore space part of the surface estate or mineral rights under traditional property law principles; (2) which federal and state agencies would permit and regulate CO_2 pipelines transporting the gas from the point of generation to the sequestration site under the existing framework for pipeline regulation; and (3) concerns over liability exposure that may hinder development of CCS technology.[77]

F. Constitutional Barriers to State Action

Two federal constitutional constraints on state action, preemption and the dormant commerce clause, have played a role in blocking state efforts to restrict GHG emissions.[78]

1. Preemption

At least two federal statutes have been invoked to argue for federal preemption of state laws affecting GHG emissions: the CAA and the Energy Policy and Conservation Act (EPCA). The CAA, while not generally preempting state regulation of stationary source emissions, does preempt state standards "relating to" the control of emissions from new motor vehicles.[79] An exception is that EPA may waive CAA preemption for vehicle emission standards in California, should that state so request,[80] whereupon states with standards identical to California's also participate in the waiver.[81] EPCA, for its part, is not directly concerned with emissions. Rather, it authorizes federal promulgation of corporate average fuel economy standards ("CAFE standards"),[82] then dictates that when a CAFE standard is in effect, a state may not regulate in a

---

[76] This section of the report was written by Adam Vann, Legislative Attorney, CRS American Law Division.

[77] For a detailed discussion of these issues, see CRS Report RL34307, *Legal Issues Associated with the Development of Carbon Dioxide Sequestration Technology*, by Adam Vann and Paul W. Parfomak. *See also* David E. Adelman and Ian J. Duncan, *The Limits of Liability in Promoting Safe Geologic Sequestration of CO₂*, 43 Envtl. L. Rptr. 10646 (2013); Will Reisinger et al., *Reconciling King Coal and Climate Change: A Regulatory Framework for Carbon Capture*, 11 Vt. J. Envtl. L. 1, 13-25 (2009).

[78] *State* constitutional constraints are not covered in this report.

[79] CAA § 209(a); 42 U.S.C. § 7543(a).

[80] CAA § 209(b); 42 U.S.C. § 7543(b).

[81] CAA § 177; 42 U.S.C. § 7507.

[82] 49 U.S.C. § 32902(a).

manner "related to" such fuel economy standards.[83] No California waiver or other waiver is authorized.

An obvious ambiguity exists as to when a state action is "relating to" or "related to" the relevant federal action, and thus preempted. For example, one case dealt with city regulations reducing the rates at which taxicab owners could lease vehicles to drivers if the vehicle did not have a hybrid engine. The court found it "likely" (the standard for obtaining a preliminary injunction) that the regulations effectively required cab owners to buy only hybrid vehicles, so that the regulations were "relating to" the control of emissions under the CAA and "related to" CAFE standards under EPCA. So finding, the court held that plaintiffs had shown a likelihood of success in showing preemption and granted a preliminary injunction.[84]

It is also unclear at what point a state's actions restricting GHG emissions are preempted as interfering with national foreign policy, given the long history of U.S. involvement in international negotiations over GHG emissions.[85] The issue has been raised in litigation.[86]

Finally, states participating in the Regional Greenhouse Gas Initiative (RGGI) have committed to finding a solution to GHG emissions from the generation of electricity imported into those states. Because the Federal Power Act creates exclusive federal control over interstate wholesale power rates,[87] the issue has been raised whether state regulation of imported electricity is consistent with federal authority. The answer must await the details of any RGGI proposal, but state regulation that does not affect interstate wholesale power rates would seem likely to survive Federal Power Act preemption challenge.[88] Close questions might arise, however, if a RGGI initiative by imposing additional costs on out-of-state power generation indirectly increased interstate wholesale rates.

2. Dormant Commerce Clause

The dormant commerce clause (DCC), a judicially created corollary of the Constitution's Commerce Clause,[89] seeks to ensure that state laws do not impermissibly thwart interstate commerce. First, the DCC imposes a difficult-to-meet, strict scrutiny test on any state law that on its face, or in practical effect, discriminates against commerce based on its out-of-state origin. Second, it applies a considerably more lenient balancing test when a state law, though not discriminating against interstate commerce, nonetheless imposes an "undue burden" on such commerce. And third, the DCC is construed to contain a categorical ban on state laws that

---

[83] 49 U.S.C. § 32919.

[84] Metropolitan Taxicab Bd. of Trade v. City of New York, 633 F. Supp. 2d 83 (S.D.N.Y.), *affirmed as to EPCA*, 615 F.3d 152 (2d Cir. 2010), *cert. denied*, 131 S. Ct. 1569 (2011).

[85] As the Supreme Court noted in *Massachusetts v. EPA*, 549 U.S. 497, 519 (2007): "Massachusetts ... cannot negotiate [a GHG] emissions treaty with China or India ...." The leading decision on foreign policy preemption is *American Insurance Ass'n v. Garamendi*, 539 U.S. 396 (2003).

[86] *See, e.g.*, Green Mountain Chrysler Plymouth Dodge v. Crombie, 508 F. Supp. 2d 295 (D. Vt. 2007) (no foreign policy preemption found of Vermont's GHG emission standards for new automobiles).

[87] 16 U.S.C. § 824(b). *See* Nantahala Power & Light Co. v. Thornburg, 476 U.S. 953, 966 (1986).

[88] *See* Shelley Welton, Michael Gerrard, and Jason Munster, *Regulating Electricity Imports into RGGI: Toward a Legal, Workable Solution* (Columbia Law School Center for Climate Change Law August 2013).

[89] U.S. Const. art. I, § 8, cl. 3.

---

regulate extraterritorially.[90] DCC issues have been raised in a variety of climate-change-related contexts.

In *Rocky Mountain Farmers Union v. Corey*, the Ninth Circuit overturned a district court decision holding that California's Low Carbon Fuel Standard transgressed the DCC.[91] The district court had focused on the Standard's limit on a fuel's "carbon intensity"—that is, the CO_2 emissions generated by the fuel's entire life cycle, including its production and transportation. This focus put fuels produced out-of-state at a disadvantage to fuels produced in-state. The Ninth Circuit, however, ruled 2-1 that no DCC violation existed. It held that treatment of a fuel based on its carbon intensity was not a facial discrimination based on the fuel's out-of-state origin. Nor did the Circuit agree with the district court's holding that the lifecycle standard regulated extraterritorially.

The opposite result, sustaining a DCC challenge, was reached by a federal district court in Minnesota. [92] This case involves a Minnesota statute under which persons in that state may not import from outside the state power from any large power plant that would increase CO_2 emissions from the generation of electricity because imported without an offset. The DCC argument of the plaintiffs was that all three DCC tests were violated: the statute discriminates against out-of-state interests, imposes undue burdens on interstate commerce, and violates the DCC's bar on extraterritorial regulation by regulating CO_2 emissions from the out-of-state production of electricity consumed in Minnesota.[93] Finding the statute to be per se invalid because it regulates extraterritorially, the court declined to reach the plaintiff's first two arguments.

Climate-change-related DCC issues also arise under California's cap-and-trade system—in particular, its requirement that importers of electricity account for their emissions. Should the northeastern states in RGGI adopt electricity import restrictions (see preceding section), the same constitutional issue would arise.[94] Yet another target of challenges might be SB 1368, a 2006 California law that set an "emission performance standard" for all long-term power contracts and baseload generation. The standard was set at 1,100 pounds of CO_2 per megawatt-hour. Since most

---

[90] Healy v. Beer Institute, Inc., 491 U.S. 324 (1989). Under the clause, a state may not "directly control[] commerce occurring wholly outside the boundaries of a State." *Id.* at 336. There seems to be some indeterminacy, however, in the reach of this extraterritoriality doctrine—that is, whether it means anything more than that a state may not formally assert its authority outside its borders. *See, e.g.*, Freedom Holdings, Inc. v. Cuomo, 624 F.3d 38, 67 (2d Cir. 2010) ("[m]ere 'upstream pricing impact' is not a violation of the dormant Commerce Clause, even if the impact is felt out-of-state where the stream originates").

[91] 730 F.3d 1070 (9th Cir. 2013), *cert. denied*, 134 S. Ct. 2875 (2014).

[92] North Dakota v. Heydinger, 2014 WL 1612331 (D. Minn. April 18, 2014).

[93] For discussion of this Minnesota case and the California case in the preceding paragraph, see Alexandra B. Klass and Elizabeth Henley, *Energy Policy, Extraterritoriality, and the Dormant Commerce Clause*, SSRN Legal Studies Research Paper Series, Research Paper No. 14-01 (2014).

[94] *See Regulating Electricity Imports, supra* note 83. The authors address one of the primary mechanisms being considered by the RGGI states for regulating imports: "an obligation on 'load-serving entities' ...—those companies responsible for supplying electricity to end-use customers—to purchase allowances to account for the emissions associated with the electricity they sell that is imported." *Id.* at 1. The authors conclude that such regulations should be found not to discriminate against out-of-state companies, hence in compliance with the dormant commerce clause. Such regulations, they argue, "are fundamentally *not* protectionist regulations—to the contrary, they impose far greater burdens on in-state generators than out-of-state generators would face." *Id.* at iv (emphasis in original). The authors add, however, that "this conclusion is subject to many caveats and nuances.... " *Id.* at iv.

of the generation that exceeds that standard is located outside California (in the coal states of Wyoming and Montana), the law might be argued to overburden out-of-state competitors.[95]

Finally, DCC objections have been judicially raised to a state's prohibition on use of out-of-state renewable energy to satisfy the state's required use of renewable energy by its utilities.[96]

G. The Public Trust Doctrine and GHG Emissions

In May 2011, a coordinated campaign of lawsuits and rulemaking petitions was initiated based on the argument that (1) the states and the federal government have a public trust responsibility to protect the atmosphere, and (2) with regard to climate change, they have failed to exercise that responsibility.[97] Either a lawsuit (about 12) or a petition (about 40) was filed in each state. The lawsuits and petitions, many filed by minors through their guardians ad litem, are being coordinated by Our Children's Trust, an Oregon nonprofit.

As background, the public trust doctrine[98] is an ancient common law principle with origins in Roman law and the Magna Carta. It asserts that certain natural resources are held by the sovereign in special status. Key aspects of that special status are that government may neither alienate public trust resources nor, more pertinent here, permit their injury by private parties. Rather, government has an affirmative duty to safeguard these resources for the benefit of the general public. The doctrine is generally a principle of state law, though there is limited recognition of a federal counterpart. After tidelands and the beds of navigable waterways, fish and wildlife are the natural resources most traditionally associated with the public trust doctrine; courts do not appear to have applied the doctrine to the atmosphere yet, as the suits and petitions here are seeking.

As for the lawsuits, each one reportedly asks the court for declaratory relief proclaiming that the atmosphere is a public trust resource and that the government in question has a fiduciary duty as trustee to protect it. Some of the suits ask for injunctive relief as well.

Thus far, the trend in the litigation results has been against the plaintiffs—state trial courts finding, for example, that the public trust doctrine does not apply to the atmosphere,[99] or that the doctrine is not recognized in the state.[100] As yet there have been no rulings that a state, pursuant to the public trust doctrine, must act to address climate change. The suit against the United States was dismissed on the ground that the public trust doctrine is a purely state law doctrine, depriving the court of subject matter jurisdiction.[101] On the other hand, some acceptance of the Our

---

[95] *See* Debra Kahn, *Traders worry that a Calif. low-carbon fuels decision could apply to electricity imports*, E&E ClimateWire (January 20, 2012).

[96] Illinois Commerce Comm'n v. Federal Energy Regulatory Comm'n, 721 F.3d 764, 776 (7th Cir. 2013) (dictum by Judge Posner).

[97] For further details, see CRS Report R41496, *Common-Law Climate Change Litigation After* American Electric Power v. Connecticut, by Robert Meltz.

[98] *See generally* Richard M. Frank, *The Public Trust Doctrine: Assessing Its Recent Past and Charting Its Future*, 45 U.C. Davis L. Rev. 665 (2012).

[99] *See, e.g.*, Aronow v. Minnesota Dep't of Pollution Control, 2012 Westlaw 4476642 (Minn. App. October 1, 2012); Fillipone v. Iowa Dep't of Natural Resources, No. 2-1005 (Iowa Ct. App. March 13, 2013).

[100] Martinez v. State of Colorado, No. 11CV4377 (Colo. D. Ct. November 7, 2011).

[101] Alec L. ex rel Loorz v. McCarthy, 561 Fed. Appx. 7 (D.C. Cir. 2014).

Children's Trust arguments has come from Texas, Arizona, and New Mexico. In Texas, the district court ruled that, owing to broad language in the state constitution, the public trust doctrine "includes all natural resources of the State," including the atmosphere, but that owing to pending litigation on whether the Texas Clean Air Act covers GHGs, the state's refusal to exercise its GHG authority was reasonable.[102] Similarly, an Arizona court accepted that the public trust doctrine is not limited to water-related issues, but, as with Texas, found other reasons to dismiss the case.[103] In New Mexico, the district court found that plaintiff's claim was not appropriate for disposition at the pleading stage and may proceed to the merits.[104] As for the rulemaking petitions, however, these have been denied in at least 27 jurisdictions.[105]

The generally negative results of the public trust litigation and petitions thus far are not surprising. As much as because the suits and petitions seek a major expansion of the public trust doctrine, courts are traditionally reluctant to obtrude into matters, such as global climate change, where there is little concrete guidance for determining liability or fashioning relief.

III. Liability for Harms Caused by Climate Change

Based on consensus predictions as to the many harms that climate change may cause, one may safely predict that liability lawsuits will be filed. This report previously mentioned the standing hurdle looming before climate change plaintiffs, especially those that are not states, and the political question hurdle. Following are some additional issues in liability actions.

A. Liability After *American Electric Power Co., Inc. v. Connecticut*

In *American Electric Power Co., Inc. v. Connecticut*,[106] the Supreme Court read the CAA to bar federal judges from imposing their own limits on GHG emissions from fossil-fuel-fired power plants, separate from those imposed by EPA under that act. More formally, the Court held that the CAA displaces any federal common law of nuisance that might ground a claim seeking judicial abatement of such emissions. However, *American Electric Power* left open two key questions. First, may those suffering climate-change impacts still assert federal common law of nuisance actions seeking not injunctive relief, as plaintiffs sought in *American Electric Power*, but rather *monetary damages*? Second, do *state law* claims, either common law or statutory, withstand *American Electric Power*, which addressed only *federal* common law claims?[107]

These questions were both answered in the negative in *Comer v. Murphy Oil Co.*[108] There, Mississippi landowners pressed state and federal tort claims (nuisance, trespass, and negligence) against numerous oil, coal, and chemical companies that allegedly emitted substantial GHGs. The

---

[102] Angela Bonser-Lain v. Texas Comm'n on Envtl. Quality, No. D-1-GN-11-002194 (Tex. D. Ct. August 2, 2012).

[103] Butler v. Brewer, No. 12-0347 (Ariz. Ct. App. March 15, 2013).

[104] Akilah Sanders-Reed v. Martinez, No. D-101-CV-2011-01514 (N.M. D. Ct. July 14, 2012).

[105] *See* http://climatelawyers.com/post/2012/02/04/Aronow-v-Minnesota-is-Dismissed-Public-Trust-Doctrine-Not-Extended-to-the-Atmosphere-in-Minnesota.aspx.

[106] 131 S. Ct. 2527 (2011).

[107] *See generally* Scott Gallisdorfer, Note, *Clean Air Act Preemption of State Common Law: Greenhouse Gas Nuisance Claims After* American Electric Power v. Connecticut, 99 Va. L. Rev. 131 (2013).

[108] 839 F. Supp. 2d 849 (S.D. Miss. 2012), *affirmed*, 718 F.3d 460 (5th Cir. 2013).

---

landowners' claims were based on property-related harms suffered as the result of Hurricane Katrina—they argued that the defendants, through their GHG emissions and resulting climate change, had contributed to warmer ocean temperatures that had intensified the hurricane, and to rising sea level that aggravated the hurricane's impacts further. They sought damages. Despite the differences from *American Electric Power*—state rather than federal claims, monetary rather than injunctive relief—the district court found that decision controlling. Here as in *American Electric Power*, the court said, the lawsuit called upon the court to determine what level of CO_2 emissions was unreasonable, a determination the Supreme Court explained had been entrusted by Congress to the EPA. So the court found the plaintiffs' "entire lawsuit" displaced by the CAA.[109] On appeal to the Fifth Circuit, the district court was affirmed based on res judicata—that is, because an earlier phase of the litigation had forever settled the justiciability issues in the case.

The other GHG decision on the monetary damages and state common law issues is *Native Village of Kivalina v. ExxonMobil Corp.*[110] In this case, Inupiat Alaska natives who will have to relocate their coastal village due to shore erosion sued 22 energy and utility companies for relocation costs. Their claim was that the defendants' GHG emissions had, by adding to climate change, contributed to the melting of sea ice that had protected the village's shores from wave erosion. Agreeing with *Comer*, the Ninth Circuit in *Kivalina* found the monetary damages claim displaced under *American Electric Power*. Disagreeing with *Comer*, the court (most clearly in a concurring opinion) left open the possibility of the village filing a state common law claim in state court, though state courts are unlikely to be any more welcoming of common law challenges to global problems than the federal courts in *Comer* and *Kivalina*.[111]

With the Fifth Circuit's dismissal in *Comer*, and the Supreme Court now having declined to review the Ninth Circuit's decision in *Kivalina*, prospects for a significant common law response to GHG emissions seem to be slim.

B. Insurance Coverage of Injury or Liability Associated with Climate Change

Federal and private insurers are well aware that if the scientific consensus is correct that climate change will bring on more frequent extreme weather events, they stand to make substantially increased payments.[112] At this time, there appear to be no insurance policies that provide explicit

---

[109] 839 F. Supp. 2d at 865.

[110] 696 F.3d 849 (9th Cir. 2012), *cert. denied*, 133 S. Ct. 2390 (2013).

[111] In a non-GHG case, the Third Circuit held that the CAA does not preempt state tort claims based on the law (common law or statutory) of the state where the pollution source is located. If a petition for certiorari is filed, the Supreme Court might find this case attractive as a vehicle for resolving the unanswered question in *American Electric Power* as to CAA displacement of state common law claims. Bell v. Cheswick Generating Station, 734 F.3d 188 (3d Cir. 2013).

[112] Evan Mills, *The Greening of Insurance*, 338 Science 1424 (December 14, 2012); Evan Lehmann, *Reinsurers press Congress to reduce U.S. risk from climate change* (E&E ClimateWire, March 2, 2012); Evan Lehmann, *Disasters, continuing to climb, inflict record insurance losses in 2011* (E&E ClimateWire, January 5, 2012); Government Accountability Office, *Climate Change: Financial Risks to Federal and Private Insurers in Coming Decades Are Potentially Significant*, GAO-07-760T (2007). For general background, see Christina M. Carroll et al., CLIMATE CHANGE AND INSURANCE (2012); Gary S. Guzy, "Insurance and Climate Change," in Michael B. Gerrard (ed.), GLOBAL CLIMATE CHANGE AND U.S. LAW (ABA 2007); Justin Pidot, Georgetown Envtl. Law and Policy Inst., *Coastal Disaster Insurance in the Era of Global Warming* (2007) (copy on file with author); Adam Riedel, *California, New York and Washington to Require Insurers to Provide Information on Climate Change Risks*, available at (continued...)

---

coverage for injuries resulting from climate change; however, there are policies that cover many of the injuries likely to be associated with climate change, "such as flood, wind, freezing, heat, earth movement, or collapse."[113]

Some issues in the vast universe of insurance-coverage litigation seem to be especially relevant to climate change. One arises from coastal hurricanes, the impacts of which may be exacerbated by climate-change-induced sea level rise. The issue is whether a particular item of hurricane damage is to be regarded as wind-caused damage or flood-caused damage. The distinction is pivotal because domestic insurance policies cover only wind damage; flood damage is insured under the National Flood Insurance Program.[114] The litigation in this wind/flooding area, such as that generated by Hurricane Katrina, is voluminous and often turns on factual questions, but also raises such issues as (1) who, insurer or insured, bears the burden of showing the portion of damage covered by the policy when both an insured (say, wind-caused) risk and a non-insured (say, flooding-caused) risk contributed;[115] (2) whether water driven by wind ("storm surge") falls outside the flooding exclusion in homeowners' policies;[116] and (3) whether the flooding exclusion covers man-made causes (e.g., negligent maintenance of levees) as well as natural ones.[117]

Another issue is whether the Commercial General Liability (CGL) policy used by businesses covers liability imposed on the insured as the result of the insured's GHG emissions, when those emissions contribute to climate-change-related damage. The only known decision on this issue is *AES Corp. v. Steadfast Ins. Co.*,[118] a ruling by the Virginia Supreme Court that the insurance company was not obligated to provide defense under its CGL policy with AES in the *Kivalina* suit,[119] because Kivalina's complaint did not allege an "occurrence."[120]

Finally, some policies, such as environmental liability or pollution policies, cover damage from "pollution." Where "pollution" is defined in policies to mean substances classified as pollutants under environmental laws, the Supreme Court decision in *Massachusetts v. EPA* may prove pivotal.[121] There, the Court held that GHG emissions are "air pollutants" under the Clean Air Act, raising the possibility that this ruling will be used to enlarge policy coverage to bring in damage traceable to GHG emissions.

(...continued)

blogs.law.columbia.edu/climate change/2012/02/06.

[113] *Guzy, supra* note 112, at 554.

[114] 42 U.S.C. §§ 4001-4029.

[115] *See, e.g.,* Bayle v. Allstate Ins. Co., 615 F.3d 350 (5th Cir. 2010).

[116] *See, e.g.,* Leonard v. Nationwide Ins. Co., 499 F.3d 419 (5th Cir. 2007).

[117] *See, e.g.,* In re Katrina Canal Breaches Litigation, 495 F.3d 191 (5th Cir. 2007).

[118] 725 S.E.2d 532 (Va. 2012).

[119] See description of this suit in text accompanying note 110 *supra*.

[120] As the court explained, an insurance company must defend its insured only when the complaint against the insured alleges facts that, if proved, fall within the risk covered by the policy. The CGL policy covers only an "occurrence," defined in the policy as an "accident." Accidents, the court said, can occur with intentional acts, such as AES's release of GHGs, but only when the alleged injury is "out of the ordinary expectation of a reasonable person." 725 S.E.2d at 536. That unexpected-injury condition was not met: Kivalina's complaint alleged that the consequences of AES's GHG emissions—the damage to the village—were not merely foreseeable, but natural and probable. Based on that allegation, there was no "accident" or "occurrence," so the CGL policy did not provide coverage and the insurance company had no duty to defend.

[121] 549 U.S. 497 (2011).

C. U.S. Liability in International Fora Based on GHG Emissions

Whether sovereign nations may be, or should be, liable under international law for failing to reduce GHG emissions within their territory has long attracted the attention of commentators[122]— and, of course, low-lying nations. However, research fails to reveal any successful effort to impose such liability.

Some principles that might be applied to a claim alleging GHG-caused injury might be taken from the international law of transboundary pollution. For example, the Restatement (Third) of Foreign Relations Law describes an international law principle under which a nation must "take such measures as may be necessary, to the extent practicable under the circumstances, to ensure that activities within its jurisdiction or control ... are conducted so as not to cause significant injury to the environment of another state."[123] Similarly, the *Trail Smelter* arbitration decision, probably the seminal ruling on state liability for transboundary pollution, declared that "[a] State owes at all times a duty to protect other States against injurious acts by individuals from within its jurisdiction."[124] Of course, as with the domestic litigation, daunting hurdles confront the international-law claimant in making the link between climate change in general and specific environmental harms, and in apportioning how much of such harms to attribute to the charged parties.

Research reveals only one climate-change-related international law action filed against the United States. In 2005, the chair of the Inuit Circumpolar Conference, on behalf of herself and all affected Inuit of the arctic regions of the United States and Canada, filed a petition against the United States with the Inter-American Commission on Human Rights, the investigative arm of the Organization of American States (OAS).[125] The petition alleged that the United States, through its failure to restrict its GHG emissions and the resultant climate change, had violated the Inuits' human rights—including their rights to their culture, to property, to the preservation of health, life, and to physical integrity. Inuit culture is described in the petition as "inseparable from the condition of [its] physical surroundings."[126] Generally, the Inter-American Commission on Human Rights is empowered to recommend measures that contribute to human rights protection, request states in urgent cases to adopt specific precautionary measures to avoid serious harm to human rights, or submit cases to the Inter-American Court of Human Rights. The United States, however, has not accepted the jurisdiction of this court, so the Inuit petition sought only to have the commission prepare a report declaring the responsibilities of the United States and recommending corrective measures.

---

[122] *See* Michael Faure et al., CLIMATE CHANGE LIABILITY (2011); Richard Lord et al. (eds.), CLIMATE CHANGE LIABILITY: TRANSNATIONAL LAW AND PRACTICE (2012); Timo Koivurova, *International Legal Avenues to Address the Plight of Victims of Climate Change*, 62 J. Envtl. L. & Litig. 269 (2007); Andrew L. Strauss, *The Legal Option: Suing the United States in International Forums for Global Warming Emissions*, 33 Envtl. L. Rptr. 10185 (2003).

[123] RESTATEMENT (THIRD) OF FOREIGN RELATIONS LAW § 601(1). *See also* Legality of the Threat or Use of Nuclear Weapons, Advisory Opinion, 1996 ICJ Reports 226, 241-242 (July 8, 1996) ("the existence of the general obligation of states to ensure that activities within their jurisdiction and control respect the environment of other states or of areas beyond national control is now part of the corpus of international law relating to the environment").

[124] Trail Smelter (U.S. v. Canada), 3 R.I.A.A. 1938, 1965 (March 11, 1941).

[125] Petition to the Inter American Commission on Human Rights Seeking Relief from Violations Resulting from Global Warming Caused by Actions and Omissions of the United States, available at http://inuitcircumpolar.com/files/uploads/icc-files/FINALPetitionICC.pdf. For detailed discussion of the petition, see Koivurova, *supra* note 122, at 285.

[126] *Id.* at 5.

In 2006, the Commission informed the petitioner that it would not process the petition "at present," explaining that "the information provided does not enable us to determine whether the alleged facts would tend to characterize a violation of rights protected by the American Declaration."[127]

IV. Climate Change-Induced Water Shortages

A. Water Scarcity and Water Rights

It is widely predicted that climate change will exacerbate water scarcity—widening arid areas and making them even drier. The future of the western United States has received substantial attention in this regard.[128] Where demand outstrips supply, the nature and flexibility of existing water rights are raised.

To be sure, water rights, mostly a creature of state law, are property of a uniquely conditional nature. Most obviously, the water rights holder does not own the water to which the right applies; the right is merely "usufructuary," that is, to *use* the water. In the western United States, water rights generally are governed by "prior appropriation" doctrine, under which the right of use is contingent on the right holder putting the water to "beneficial use," and is further subject to common law or statutory limits based on the public trust doctrine and the doctrine of reasonable use. With regard to "reasonable use," the California Constitution, as an example, declares that the "unreasonable use or unreasonable method of use of water be prevented," a doctrine that is self-executing and evolving.[129] Appropriation doctrine is a "first in time, first in right" system under which inadequate supply results in junior-in-time appropriators having their water cut before senior-in-time appropriators. At bottom, of course, all water rights depend on the natural supply.

Despite the conditionality of water rights, it remains to be seen how much latitude government has to respond to periods of water scarcity without effecting a Fifth Amendment taking of such rights.[130] In the short term, government response might take the form of cutbacks in the consumption of vested water rights holders to accommodate critical public needs; in the long term, legislative or judicial change in the water rights regime might be in order.[131] It is also unclear to what extent appropriation doctrine states may allow water rights holders to transfer water rights, generally favored by scholars as promoting more efficient outcomes and the

---

[127] Letter from Ariel E. Dulitzky, Ass't Executive Sec'y, Inter-American Commission on Human Rights, to Sheila Watt-Cloutier (November 16, 2006), available at http://graphics8 nytimes.com/packages/pdf/science/16commissionletter.pdf. The "American Declaration" referred to by the Commission is the American Declaration of the Rights and Duties of Man, OAS Res. XXX, available at http://www1.umn.edu/humanrts/oasinstr/zoas2dec.htm.

[128] See the discussion of the possible effects of climate change on water availability in the western United States in Priyanka Sundareshan, *Using the Transfer of Water Rights as a Climate Change Adaptation Strategy: Comparing the United States and Australia*, 27 Ariz. J. Int'l & Comp. L. 911, 920-921 (2010).

[129] Cal Const. art. 10, § 2 (describing the principles of beneficial use and reasonableness as "self-executing"); State Water Resources Control Bd. v. Forni, 126 Cal. Rptr. 851 (Cal. App. 1976) (noting that "[w]hat is a [reasonable and] beneficial use at one time may, because of changed conditions, become a waste of water at a later time").

[130] *See* A Dan Tarlock, *Takings, Water Rights, and Climate Change*, 36 Vt. L. Rev. 731, 732 (2012) ("when legislatures, administrative agencies, and courts shift titles and reduce existing rights to share [water] resources more equitably among competing demands, there will be takings challenges").

[131] Judicial change in the water rights regime raises the issue of "judicial takings." *See* text accompanying note 149 *infra*.

---

achieving of environmental goals.[132] One writer has noted that in the West, the explosive population growth of recent decades has often occurred in communities with only junior water rights. Senior water rights holders often include older municipalities, mining, and agriculture.[133] The question then arises whether reasonable use and other doctrines qualifying appropriation water rights can address the difficult situation of new communities being starved for water while senior appropriators endure little or no reduction in water supplies.

States have evolved a variety of additional mechanisms for allocating water among rights holders in times of scarcity. Many states exempt certain "domestic" uses of water (e.g., for stock watering, home use, or lawn watering) from the general permit scheme. If climate change produces more droughts, conflicts will increase between exempted users and those with appropriation rights, especially senior appropriators. In some cases, the ability of an exempted user to leapfrog over the rights of senior appropriators may be held subject to payment of compensation under the constitutional right to compensation for the taking of property.[134]

The above issues also are likely to arise with groundwater, which, as with surface water, is usually held by the landowner under a right of use only, not outright ownership.[135] A recent Texas Supreme Court decision, however, adopted the minority view of outright ownership, analogizing to ownership of underlying oil and gas. The court reassured the state that conservation of groundwater, in this instance from the Edwards Aquifer, still can be done without takings as long as the problems of limited water supply "are shared by the public, not foisted onto a few."[136] However, in the first Texas case following this decision, a court concluded that the state's permitting system for groundwater withdrawals from the Edwards Aquifer effected a regulatory taking of the plaintiffs' land.[137]

B. Water Diversion and Delivery Cutbacks

Periods of low precipitation, as may be more frequent in the future due to climate change, have generated several court decisions where the conflict was between the water needs of the public and those of fish in streams. These decisions resolved claims of Fifth Amendment takings of water rights and claims of government breach of water-supply contracts based on cutbacks in the amount of water delivered from federal water projects—as demanded by the Endangered Species Act[138] and the Central Valley Improvement Act.[139] A key issue in these cases has been whether the

---

[132] Sundareshan, *supra* note 128, at 923-925. *See also* Mark Squillace, *Water Transfers for a Changing Climate*, 53 Nat. Res. J. 55 (2013).

[133] Joel Smith et al., Georgetown Climate Center, *Adaptation Case Studies in the Western United States* at 22 (2011) (writing with specific reference to Colorado's prior appropriation doctrine).

[134] *See, e.g.*, Bassinger v. Taylor, 164 P. 522, 523 (Idaho 1917).

[135] Again using California as our example, that state's Supreme Court has explained that "overlying water rights are usufructuary only, and while conferring the legal right to use the water that is superior to all other users, confer no private right of ownership in public waters." City of Barstow v. Mohave Water Agency, 5 P.3d 853, 860 n.7 (Cal. 2000). An illustrative decision on a takings challenge to a county restriction on withdrawal of groundwater (not, so far as appears, for climate change reasons) is *Allegretti & Co. v. County of Imperial*, 42 Cal. Rptr. 3d 122 (Cal. App. 2006) (no physical or regulatory taking caused by 12,000 acre-feet per year limit imposed by county in groundwater withdrawal permit).

[136] Edwards Aquifer Auth. v. Day, 369 S.W.3d 814 (Tex. 2012). The case was remanded for further development of the factual record, as needed to apply the regulatory takings test.

[137] Edwards Aquifer Auth. v. Bragg, 2013 WL 5989430 (Tex. App. Nov. 13, 2013).

[138] Tulare Lake Basin Water Storage Dist. v. United States, 49 Fed. Cl. 313 (2001) (holding that taking occurred); (continued...)

---

taking claim is to be analyzed by the court as a physical taking of the water, or as a regulatory taking of use rights in the water. The distinction matters a great deal. In general, a plaintiff's litigation prospects are substantially improved if the court adopts a physical takings framework, thus the physical versus regulatory takings issue has been hard fought in the courts. Currently, it appears that when the government requires a *physical diversion of the water* away from the plaintiff's desired use (as to operate a fish ladder), the plaintiff-friendly physical taking approach is triggered.[140] But, it would appear, not otherwise.

Another issue has been the role of doctrines that qualify water rights—principally, public trust and reasonable use.[141] Do these doctrines allow the government to set supervening public priorities for fish preservation as part of rights it retains when conferring water rights? If the government retains such rights, no taking claim can succeed, for the water rights holder cannot be found to have suffered a taking of a right he or she never acquired.

V. Sea Level Rise and Extreme Precipitation

A. Effect of Sea Level Rise on the Beachfront Owner's Property Line

Sea level rise generally causes the boundary between land and water to move landward.[142] The common law has long had to deal with such shifting boundaries—in particular, with who owns land newly dry or newly submerged. The rule, dating back to Roman times, turns on whether the land-water boundary shift occurred slowly or quickly. When land-water boundaries shift *gradually and imperceptibly*—"so slowly that one could not see the change occurring"[143]—the ownership boundary shifts with it. Thus, in the case of "accretion," defined as the gradual depositing of alluvion (sand, sediment, or other deposits) so as to enlarge one's tract, the owner of the tract becomes the happy owner of the accreted area as well. The shore owner may be less pleased, however, with "erosion," the gradual and imperceptible boundary shift towards land

---

(...continued)

Klamath Irrigation Dist. v. United States, 635 F.3d 505 (Fed. Cir. 2011) (remanding taking and breach claims for further proceedings); Casitas Municipal Water Dist. v. United States, 708 F.3d 1340 (Fed. Cir. 2013) (taking claim held not ripe).

[139] Stockton East Water Dist. v. United States, 101 Fed. Cl. 352 (2011) (dismissing taking claim); 2013 Westlaw 751280, 766531 (Fed. Cl. February 28, 2013) (awarding contract damages).

[140] Casitas Municipal Water Dist. v. United States, 543 F.3d 1276 (Fed. Cir. 2008).

[141] As explained in the *Casitas* remand, 102 Fed. Cl. at 455, with reference to the state of California:

> Under the public trust doctrine, state agencies have the responsibility to protect trust resources associated with California's waterways, such as navigation, fisheries, recreation, ecological preservation, and related beneficial uses. .... Similarly, the reasonable use doctrine prohibits the waste, unreasonable use, unreasonable method of use, and unreasonable method of diversion of water. (citations omitted)

[142] In some locations, sea level relative to the adjacent land has "fallen" because the land has risen more than the sea level. Land may rise once relieved of the massive weight of retreating glaciers as the result of climate change, natural and human-induced. Cornelia Dean, *As Alaska Glaciers Melt, It's Land That's Rising*, New York Times, May 19, 2009, at A1.

[143] Stop the Beach Renourishment, Inc. v. Florida Dep't of Envtl. Prot., 560 U.S. 702, 708 (2010).

---

when former upland is submerged. As with accretion, the property line moves—landward this time.[144]

In contrast with accretion and erosion, *sudden* shifts in the land-water boundary, known regardless of direction as "avulsion," do not shift ownership lines. A classic avulsive event is a hurricane that abruptly shifts the mean high water mark on a beach either seaward or landward. In this case, the property line between the owner of the intertidal zone and permanently submerged lands (typically the state in trust for the public) and the owner of uplands beyond the high water mark (typically a private entity) does not move.[145]

A key question is whether movement in the land-water boundary owing to climate-change-caused sea level rise is fast enough to be avulsive, leaving the property line unmoved, or gradual enough to be erosion, reducing the shoreowner's property.[146] No case law on the point exists, but scholars predict that courts will favor the latter. One scholar asserts: "The rising sea level [from climate change] is neither gradual like traditional accretion, erosion, or reliction; nor is it sudden and violent like traditional avulsion. We are facing a historically distinct situation that is not a good factual fit with the [traditional common law] rules."[147] Nonetheless, he stresses that in light of the public interest in maintaining authority over water-covered areas (e.g., for regulating navigation) and the adjacent foreshore, the judicial presumption in the case law strongly leans toward accretion and erosion, with their migrating property lines.[148] Likewise, two other scholars predict that "in most instances sea level rise [from climate change] will transform private property into public property as sea waters cover formerly dry land."[149] Courts are unlikely to view this private-to-public change as a Fifth Amendment taking of property rights, since property is held subject to traditional common law principles.

Case law authority also suggests that public trust ownership of coastal submerged lands and the adjacent intertidal zone (between low and high water mark) expands automatically when erosion occurs. That is, no legal process is required. In *McQueen v. South Carolina Coastal Council*, for example, that state's high court decreed that under state law, wetlands created by the encroachment of navigable tidal water belong to the state—that is, are public trust property. That such lands were upland when acquired and that the tidelands were subsequently created by the

---

[144] *See, e.g.*, City of Long Branch v. Jui Yung Liu, 4 A.3d 542, 550 (N.J. 2010).

[145] For extended discussion of the law of accretion and avulsion, see Joseph L. Sax, *The Accretion/Avulsion Puzzle: Its Past Revealed, Its Future Proposed*, 23 Tulane Envtl. L. J. 305 (2010), and James G. Titus, *Rising Seas, Coastal Erosion, and the Takings Clause: How to Save Wetlands and Beaches Without Hurting Property Owners*, 57 Md. L. Rev. 1279 (1998).

[146] Identifying the portion of coastal erosion attributable to sea level rise may be a challenge. One writer notes: "In many Gulf of Mexico states, ... the projected rate of beach loss due to sea level rise is overwhelmed by the current background rate of erosion." Donna M. Christie, *Sea Level Rise and Gulf Beaches: The Specter of Judicial Takings*, 26 J. Land Use & Envtl. L. 313, 314 (2011).

[147] *See* Joseph L. Sax, *Some Unorthodox Thoughts About Rising Sea Levels, Beach Erosion and Property Rights*, 11 Vt. J. Envtl. L. 641, 645 (2010).

[148] Joseph L. Sax, *supra* note 145. The presumption favoring accretion and erosion, Prof. Sax notes, "has largely relegated the avulsion rule to a minor role...." 23 Tulane Envtl. L. J. at 351.

[149] J. Peter Byrne and Jessica Grannis, *Coastal Retreat Measures*, in Michael B. Gerrard and Katrina F. Kuh, (eds.), THE LAW OF ADAPTATION TO CLIMATE CHANGE: U.S. AND INTERNATIONAL ASPECTS (ABA 2012). *See also* J. Peter Byrne, *The Cathedral Engulfed: Sea-level Rise, Property Rights, and Time*, 73 La. L. Rev. 69, 80 (2012) ("Sea level rise is incremental, and therefore, corresponding land loss will be subject to the doctrine of accretion.... ").

rising of tidal water, said the court, cannot defeat the state's presumptive title to the tidelands.[150] As well, the court held, the state incurs no takings liability.

As long as state courts are able to ground such extensions of public trust lands in traditional common law, no Fifth Amendment taking from beachfront property owners is likely to be discerned. As noted, title to coastal property (or any other property) is assumed to be qualified by traditional common law principles, and public trust doctrine certainly falls into this category.[151] On the other hand, if courts use sea level rise as an occasion to expand public trust doctrine beyond its traditional state-law parameters or to otherwise shrink littoral rights, the possibility of a so-called "judicial taking" may arise. This novel concept, that *courts* may effect takings just as other branches of government do, received a non-precedential boost in 2010 when a Supreme Court plurality proposed that "[i]f a legislature *or a court* declares that what was once an established right of private property no longer exists, it has taken that property."[152] As yet, however, no court has ever found a judicial taking in a final decision.

B. "Rolling" Beach Easements and Removal Requirements

Cases out of Texas and North Carolina illustrate the constitutional issues that may be raised in the future by landward migration of beaches due to climate-change-induced sea level rise.

Severance v. Patterson[153] deals with the Texas Open Beaches Act, which imposes a public-access easement on the state's beaches extending landward to the dune vegetation line. The lower Texas courts had long construed this access easement to "roll"—that is, to migrate with movements in the dune vegetation line. The consequence is that landward movement of the vegetation line may result in private land, including improved parcels, being newly encumbered by the easement. Under the act, the state may then order the improvement (e.g., a house) removed, although some compensation is provided for removal expenses. Carol Severance bought two houses behind the vegetation line, only to have Hurricane Ike a few months later move the line landward of her houses—making them subject to removal orders. She asserted Fifth Amendment takings and Fourth Amendment unreasonable seizure claims.

The Fifth Circuit found the taking claim unripe, but certified questions to the Texas Supreme Court as to Severance's Fourth Amendment claim. In its answers, the Texas Supreme Court narrowed the circumstances when the public access easement rolls.[154] It concluded that "[a]lthough existing public easements in the dry beach of Galveston's West Beach are dynamic, as natural forces cause the vegetation and the mean high tide lines to move gradually and

---

[150] 580 S.E.2d 116 (S.C. 2003). *See also City of Long Branch*, 4 A.3d at 550 ("[u]nder the common law, the owner of oceanfront property takes title to dry land added by accretion, but loses to the State title over land that becomes tidally flowed as a result of erosion"); Bollay v. California Office of Administrative Law, 122 Cal. Rptr. 3d 490, 493 (Cal. App. 2011) ("the mean high tide line may change over time, affecting the seaward boundary of property along the coast").

[151] *See, e.g.,* Robin K. Craig, *Public Trust and Public Necessity Defenses to Takings Liability for Sea Level Rise Responses on the Gulf Coast*, 26 J. Land Use & Envtl. L. 395 (2011).

[152] Stop the Beach Renourishment, Inc. v. Florida Dep't of Envtl. Prot., 560 U.S. 702, 704 (2010) (emphasis in original). *See generally* Christie, *supra* note 142. As noted by Justice Kennedy in his *Stop the Beach Renourishment* concurring opinion, the Due Process Clause also constrains state courts from substantially reducing property rights by arbitrary or irrational decision.

[153] 566 F.3d 490 (5th Cir. 2009), *on answers to certified questions*, 682 F.3d 360 (5th Cir. 2012).

[154] 370 S.W.3d 705 (Tex. 2012).

---

imperceptibly, these easements do not spring or roll landward … as a result of avulsive events." In so ruling, the court reversed the decades-old interpretation of the Texas Open Beaches Act in the lower state courts, which had allowed the public access easement to roll no matter how abrupt the movement in the vegetation line. Also important, the Texas court ruling raises again the question asked in Section IV.A. as to whether climate-change-caused sea level rise should be considered gradual or avulsive.[155]

Similar litigation exists in North Carolina. There, the vegetation line moved from the seaward to landward side of homes by gradual beach erosion, rather than a hurricane. The consequence was that the town ordered the homes' demolition, under an ordinance declaring structures on oceanfront beaches to be nuisances—and asserting a public trust in both the wet and dry sand beach. The two takings claims filed (one as a counter-claim) have yet to be finally resolved.[156]

Still another example of law anticipating landward migration of beaches are the coastal sand dune rules promulgated by a Maine state agency under that state's Natural Resources Protection Act.[157] Similar to the Texas statute and North Carolina ordinance above, the Maine rules instruct that if the shoreline recedes such that a coastal wetland extends to any part of a structure for six months, the structure must be removed.[158] The rules also bar a project in a coastal sand dune system "if, within 100 years, the project may … be eroded as a result of changes in the shoreline such that the project is likely to be severely damaged after allowing for a two foot rise in sea level over 100 years."[159]

C. Shifting Floodplain Designations

Sea level rise and extreme rains born of climate change may cause lands not formerly subject to flooding to become so. Land use planners have long encountered resistance updating floodplain designations because such a designation alerts potential buyers that a parcel is vulnerable, possibly reducing the parcel's market value. It is unlikely, however, that a floodplain designation could, in itself, result in enough value loss to constitute a Fifth Amendment regulatory taking of a property.[160]

---

[155] The Fifth Circuit remanded *Severance* to the district court for further proceedings on the Fourth Amendment unreasonable seizure claim consistent with the Texas Supreme Court's answers to the certified questions. 682 F.3d 360 (5th Cir. 2012).

[156] Sansotta v. Town of Nags Head, 724 F.3d 533 (4th Cir. 2013) (holding taking claim ripe); Town of Nags Head v. Toloczko, 728 F.3d 391 (4th Cir. 2013) (same holding on different grounds). In 2012, a North Carolina court held that the public trust doctrine was a state doctrine that could only be asserted by the state, not the town of Nags Head. Town of Nags Head v. Cherry, Inc., 723 S.E.2d 156 (N.C. Ct. App.), *rev. denied*, 733 S.E.2d 85 (N.C. 2012). Hence, the takings claims in these cases, based on the now-rescinded demolition order, presumably will be litigated as *temporary* takings claims.

[157] 38 Me. Rev. Stat. Ann. §§ 480-A through 480-HH.

[158] Me. Dep't of Envtl. Prot. Admin. Code ch. 355, § 10.A.

[159] *Id.* at § 5.C.

[160] *See, e.g.*, Strother v. City of Rockwall, 358 S.W.3d 462 (Tex. App. 2012) (taking claim based on redesignation of land as floodplain defeated by, among other reasons, fact that land continued to be used for rental).

D. Issues Related to Levees and Dams

Damage from climate-change-caused extreme weather or sea level rise may require courts in the future to clarify federal liabilities in connection with the design, construction, and operation of levees and dams by the Army Corps of Engineers. The extensive litigation following the breaching and overtopping of the levees protecting New Orleans during Hurricane Katrina may be a harbinger of climate-change-related litigation.

Two statutes make clear that the United States' tort liability for harms from extreme weather or sea level rise is likely to be limited when based on levee/dam design, construction, and operation.[161] Under section 3 of the Flood Control Act, "[no] liability of any kind shall attach to or rest upon the United States for any damage from or by flood waters at any place...."[162] Under the Federal Tort Claims Act, no tort action can be maintained against the United States if based on a federal official's exercise of a "discretionary function"—meaning a decision where there is room for policy judgment and discretion.[163] This includes the large majority of decisions in connection with the design, construction, and operation of dams and levees. For example, the Fifth Circuit, addressing a Corps of Engineers shipping channel (with levees) that had the effect of channeling Hurricane Katrina storm surge to New Orleans, found the Corps not liable in tort for the resulting harm.[164] One or the other of the two liability exemptions above applied to each claim of injury.

Shifting from torts to takings, the picture becomes cloudier. On the one hand, the government is not responsible for climate-change-related flooding that would have occurred had the government not constructed the levee or dam.[165] Thus, installation of protective measures such as levees and dams "does not constitute the Government a taker of all lands not fully and wholly protected."[166] For example, a takings claim based on Katrina-related damage to New Orleans, alleging the Corps' failure to adequately design, build, or maintain adequately its levees protecting the city, was rejected.[167] The government, said the court, was not the cause of the damage. Even if the government project inflicts slight damage on a property owner in one respect, it is not a taking if the project "actually confer[s] great benefits when measured in the whole."[168]

On the other hand, significant flood-related damage that would not have happened in the absence of the levee or dam is a potential taking—and, in contrast with torts, any discretion afforded government officials would not be a defense. Moreover, the Supreme Court recently repudiated the long-standing case law that only government-caused flooding that is either permanent or at

---

[161] *See generally* CRS Report RL34131, *Flood Damage Related to Army Corps of Engineers Projects: Selected Legal Issues*, by Cynthia Brougher; David M. Stein, *Flood of Litigation: Theories of Liability of Government Entities for Damages Resulting from Levee Breaches*, 52 Loy. L. Rev. 1335 (2006).

[162] 33 U.S.C. § 702c.

[163] 28 U.S.C. § 2680(a).

[164] In re Katrina Canal Breaches Litigation, 696 F.3d 436 (5th Cir. 2012), *cert. denied*, 133 S. Ct. 2855 (2013).

[165] United States v. Sponenbarger, 308 U.S. 256, 265 (1939).

[166] *Id.*

[167] Nicholson v. United States, 77 Fed. Cl. 605 (2007) (United States' failure to adequately design, build, or maintain flood protection system in New Orleans before and after Hurricane Katrina did not effect taking; rather, property damage was due to flooding caused by storm surge and such flooding was not the direct, natural, or probable result of the flood protection system).

[168] *Sponenbarger*, 308 U.S. at 266.

least "intermittent but inevitably recurring" can be a taking (and can otherwise be only a tort). Now, after *Arkansas Game & Fish Comm'n v. United States*,[169] even temporary floods, if "repeated," may be takings—depending on various factors set out by the Court.[170] Moreover, the decision may well extend to *non-repeated* temporary floods—even single ones—depending on how one reads it. Whether *Arkansas* extends to non-repeated temporary floods is currently in litigation, and has important implications for one-time intentional releases of water from levees or dams that may be necessitated by extreme weather events due to climate change. Alternatively, the Corps of Engineers, which operates many water-control facilities, may find itself buying more flowage easements, giving it the legal right to flood private land.

A final levee-related legal issue is suggested by a news article describing opposition of residents in Virginia's Middle Peninsula to planners' proposal to rezone land for use as a dike against rising water, and noting that "[o]utside of greater New Orleans, Hampton Roads is at the biggest risk from sea-level rise of any area its size in the United States."[171] The specter of takings claims looms if the rezoning results in the severe devaluation of parcels, or is analyzed as a physical taking based on the building of the dike.

E. Failure to Take Preventive Measures

The scientific consensus that climate change will lead to further sea level rise raises the issue whether governments can be held liable for failing to act to avert the harmful impacts of such rise. Generally, failure to act cannot be the basis of a taking claim. But when a city fails to act on a hazard that is specific and well understood, negligence may lie. Thus, in one case with relevance to future heavy rains from climate change, the court held that allegations that a city was aware of the potential for overflow from the city landfill's retention ponds, and its subsequent failure to take measures to prevent such overflow, did not state a taking claim, but did properly assert negligence.[172]

VI. Other Adaptation Responses to Climate Change

The previous section touched on a few adaptation measures specifically related to sea level rise. This section continues with additional adaption measures that raise legal issues.[173]

---

[169] 133 S. Ct. 511 (2012).

[170] At the same time, the Court suggested that proving a taking based on temporary flooding would be an uphill climb: "To reject a categorical bar to temporary-flooding takings claims ... is scarcely to credit all, or even many, such claims." *Id.* at 521.

[171] Darryl Fears, "Climate change fight intensifies in Virginia," Wash. Post December 18, 2011, at A3.

[172] City of El Paso v. Ramirez, 349 S.W.3d 181 (Tex. App. 2011). *See generally* Annot., *Liability for overflow or escape of water from reservoir, ditch, or artificial pond*, 169 ALR 517.

[173] In a definitive study of possible regulatory adaptations to sea level rise, the following are listed as possible "regulatory tools": zoning and overlay zones, floodplain regulations, building codes and resilient design, setbacks/buffers, conditional development and exactions, rebuilding restrictions, subdivisions and cluster development, hard-armoring permits, soft-armoring permits, and rolling coastal management / rolling easement statutes. Jessica Grannis, Georgetown Climate Center, *Adaptation Tool Kit, Sea-Level Rise and Coastal Land Use: How Governments Can Use Land Use Practices to Adapt to Sea-Level Rise* (2011).

A. Beach Issues

1. Armoring

Shoreline "armoring"—seawalls, revetments, rip-rap, bulkheads, and manmade sand dunes[174]— has obvious relevance to climate-change-caused sea level rise. The definition of armoring in the Florida administrative code is as good as any: "a manmade structure designed to either prevent erosion of the upland property or protect eligible structures from the effects of coastal wave and current action."[175] The right to erect shore defense structures on one's property has long-standing common law imprimatur, yet the practice has its detractors. Seawalls, for example, have been said to deflect waves onto other beaches, causing sand to be scoured away, and also to cut off the natural supply of sand to the beach from the sand dune behind the wall.

As a result of these problems, some states prohibit armoring on oceanfront properties, allowing the natural landward migration of the land-water boundary caused by sea level rise.[176] Such natural migration of the boundary allows the creation of new, ecologically valuable wetlands to replace those lost to sea level rise, and the expansion of public trust lands. An obvious issue, however, is whether these and other consequences of anti-armoring laws (such as collapsing homes) trench on private property rights in a manner that must be compensated as a taking. Though the issue is certainly unresolved by the limited relevant litigation, the balance of arguments seems to tip against a taking. Most obviously, the harm to the littoral owner likely would be viewed by courts as resulting from sea level rise, not the armoring restriction.[177]

A taking claim was rejected, logically enough, where the shore owner proposed armoring on public trust lands. The case is *McQueen v. South Carolina Coastal Council,*[178] in which the state denied the owner of a tract along a manmade canal permission to build a seawall and to backfill. Even though without the seawall the tract was assumed to be unbuildable and have zero value, no taking of plaintiff's property was found to have occurred. As the court saw it, plaintiff's land had largely reverted to public-trust tideland belonging to the state by the time his application was denied. Thus, the seawall permission denial took nothing plaintiff had at the time of his application. Recall the earlier discussion of shifting public trust in connection with this case in Section IV.A.

In the absence of armoring restrictions, one can expect sea level rise to cause more beachfront landowners to install defensive structures. As a result, questions as to liability for harm to neighboring tracts may be raised more often. A hoary common law principle, the "common

---

[174] In this report, "armoring" does not include levees erected for flood protection, though some writers would extend the term that far. Levees are treated separately in Section IV.D.

[175] Fla. Admin. Code R. § 63B-33.002(5).

[176] Other states regulate seawalls short of outright prohibition, at least where the seawall is to be located seaward of the mean high water mark. *See, e.g.,* Sams v. Connecticut Dep't of Envtl. Prot., 308 Conn. 359 (2013) (seawall built seaward of high water mark without required permit must be removed as statutorily declared nuisance); *California caps on seawall permits prompt outcry, lawsuits,* E & E News (May 28, 2013).

[177] *See, e.g.,* Shell Island Homeowners Ass'n, Inc. v. Tomlinson, 517 S.E.2d 406, 415 (N.C. App. 1999) (rejecting taking challenge to state anti-armoring statute on ground that "naturally occurring phenomena are the primary causes of any loss sustained by plaintiffs"). For a fuller recitation of the takings arguments pro and con with respect to anti-armoring statutes, see J. Peter Byrne, *Rising Seas and Common Law Baselines: A Comment on Regulatory Takings Discourse Concerning Climate Change,* 11 Vt. J. Envtl. L. 625, 636-638 (2010).

[178] 580 S.E.2d 116 (S.C. 2003).

---

enemy doctrine," holds that one may erect defenses against the sea even though doing so may cause water to beat with added force against adjoining lands and require the adjoining landowner to also erect defenses.[179] Many states, however, have moved away from the common enemy doctrine toward a rule of reasonableness, under which liability for harm to others is avoided only when the interference with the flow of surface waters is "reasonable," a term that could benefit from judicial clarification.[180]

Do armoring structures block the landward shift of the line between public and private ownership, typically the mean high water mark, when that mark reaches such a structure? In *United States (Lummi Nation) v. Milner*,[181] the Ninth Circuit said no; the ownership line continues to move as if the armoring structure had not been built. While the upland owner has the right to erect structures on his or her property to defend against erosion and storm damage, the tideland owner has "a vested right to the ambulatory boundary and to the tidelands they would gain if the boundary were allowed to ambulate."[182] In short, the upland owner "[does] not have the right to permanently fix the property boundary" absent the tideland owner's consent.[183] The court pointed out that its ruling might have limited applicability, given that the tideland owner here was an Indian tribe and its federal trustee, rather than the state as in the usual case. This allowed the federal court to create federal common law, while most such disputes over tideland/upland boundaries are handled by state courts under state law. One commentator notes that "[t]he decision, if applied generally, might make many homes now behind seawalls trespassers on state property."[184]

Different issues arose when it is the *government*, not a private beachfront owner, that is pushing for armoring. In a high-profile case, a New Jersey municipality condemned an easement to erect a 22-foot-high dune on private beachfront property, to protect a barrier island from storms. The intermediate appellate court held that the jury's $375,000 compensation award, largely for the dune's partial blockage of the property owner's ocean view, was not to be reduced by the storm-protection benefit conferred on the owner. Under well-established law, the court said, compensation awarded a condemnee is offset only by benefits of the project specific to the condemnee ("special benefits"), not those enjoyed by the community at large ("general benefits"). The benefit conferred by the dune was protection of the island from storms—in the court's view, a general benefit, hence not an offset. The New Jersey Supreme Court reversed, saying that the distinction between general and special benefits should be abandoned.[185] The only consideration, it said, was whether the benefit to the landowner had an ascertainable effect on the land's market value. On that new standard, plaintiffs settled for one dollar—and, in a case brought by similarly situated land owners in the same municipality, a jury awarded $300.[186]

---

[179] United States (Lummi Nation) v. Milner, 583 F.3d 1174, 1189 (9th Cir. 2009), *citing* Revell v. People, 52 N.E. 1052, 1059 (Ill. 1898).

[180] *See generally* Wendy B. Davis, *Reasonable Use Has Become the Common Enemy*, 9 Alb. L. Envtl. Outlook J. 1, 9-10 (2004); William B. Stoebuck and Dale A. Whitman, THE LAW OF PROPERTY 432-433 (3d ed. 2000).

[181] 583 F.3d 1174 (9th Cir. 2009).

[182] *Id.* at 1189-1190.

[183] *Id.* at 1190.

[184] Joseph L. Sax, *Some Unorthodox Thoughts About Rising Sea Levels, Beach Erosion, and Property Rights*, 11 Vt. J. Envtl. L. 641, 642 n.7 (2010).

[185] Borough of Harvey Cedars v. Karan, 70 A.3d 524, 541 (N.J. 2013).

[186] *See* http://www.app.com/story/news/local/southern-ocean-county/2014/06/30/dune-easment-harvey-cedars-ocean-county/11814891/.

The low dollar amounts received by the landowners in these New Jersey cases implicitly acknowledged that the benefit to the owners of soft armoring was, in terms of property value, roughly comparable to any reduction caused to such value, as by blocking ocean views. By lowering government costs, these small awards remove a possible threat to certain state measures to protect coastal communities from storms and sea level rise.

2. Renourishment

Adding sand back to eroded beaches or building up beaches, often called beach "nourishment" or "renourishment," may be increasingly resorted to as climate change progresses and sea level rises. In the near term (but unlikely beyond), repairing the ravages of storms may be preferable to the difficulties of moving existing coastal population inland. Even Members of Congress who generally seek to limit federal spending have strongly supported Corps of Engineers beach restoration projects where the local economy depends on attractive beaches.[187]

The Supreme Court, too, has turned its attention recently to beach renourishment projects. In *Stop the Beach Renourishment, Inc. v. Florida Dep't of Environmental Protection*,[188] the Court confronted a Florida beach renourishment project that had provoked objection from a handful of the affected beachfront property owners. Those owners insisted that by adding a strip of state-owned beach in front of their eroded privately owned beach, the state had effected a Fifth Amendment taking of two of their littoral property rights: the right to ownership of future accreted land and the right to direct contact with the water. The Supreme Court held unanimously that the Florida Supreme Court had properly found no taking, since the shore owners had not shown that these littoral rights were superior to the state's right to fill in its submerged land. Note that the restored beach belonged to the state: "Florida law as it stood before the decision below allowed the state to fill in its own seabed, and the resulting sudden exposure of previously submerged land was treated like an avulsion for purposes of ownership."[189] Avulsions, recall, do not move ownership boundaries.

While *Stop the Beach Renourishment* was a victory for beach renourishment efforts, the decision turned on Florida case law precedent that may not be replicated in other states. Thus, legal challenges by littoral owners to beach restoration projects can be expected to continue.[190] Suffice it to say that if the restored portion of a beach must be privately owned to avoid takings compensation, states are unlikely to commit public funds to such restoration.[191]

---

[187] Evan Lehmann, *Conservative lawmakers, protecting their beaches, also adapt to climate change* (E&E ClimateWire February 10, 2012).

[188] 560 U.S. 702 (2010).

[189] *Id.* at 2611.

[190] *See, e.g.*, Lynnhaven Dunes Condominium Ass'n v. City of Virginia Beach, 733 S.E.2d 911 (Va. 2012) (city-built strip of restored beach effected taking of association's riparian right of accretion).

[191] A related instance of state resistance to funding beach restoration occurred in Texas as the result of the state supreme court's decision in *Severance v. Patterson*. As explained more fully in text accompanying notes 132 and 133, the court ruled that the state's public beach access easement, where it exists, does not "roll" (migrate) following sudden movements of the beach vegetation line, as following a hurricane—only following gradual movements of the vegetation line. In response, the Texas General Land Office has said that it "will not provide grant funds for erosion projects on private property without a rolling easement that grants public access to the beach." Texas General Land Office, *Severance v. Patterson: Frequently Asked Questions*, available at http://www.glo.texas.gov/what-we-do/caring-for-the-coast/_documents/open-beaches/faq-open-beaches.pdf.

Because the Florida and U.S. supreme courts found no property rights impaired in *Stop the Beach Renourishment*, they had no occasion to clarify how the *benefit* to the beachfront property owner from renourishment might factor into the taking analysis. This is a key question if the costs of beach renourishment, or at least protective sand dunes built by the government on private property, are to be affordable—an offset to the compensation owed the property owner based on the benefits he reaps from the government action might greatly reduce the amount owed.

In the previous section on armoring, a state court decision approving the reduction of monetary awards to beachfront property owners on the basis of a project's storm protection benefits was described. Similarly, a North Carolina court found a zero-dollar offer to a beachfront landowner adequate in connection with a beach renourishment project (though subject to final determination in an eminent domain proceeding). The court cited the project's benefits to the landowner as adequate compensation.[192]

B. "Managed Retreat"—Moving Development Inland

Levees, armoring, and beach restoration, discussed above, have long been well-understood techniques, widely supported by landowners if not by environmentalists. Given sea level rise of the magnitude predicted from climate change, however, the long-term viability of such structural protections seems dubious.[193] Attention is shifting instead toward "managed retreat"— government actions that discourage new development in disaster-prone areas (proactive retreat) or reconstruction following such disasters (reactive retreat).[194] When that discouragement takes the form of outright prohibition on development—rather than merely removal of development incentives—the taking issue rises yet again.[195] Takings concerns loom as well with regulations that merely *have the effect* of an outright prohibition as applied to a specific parcel of land—for example, minimum distance from the water requirements applied to small tracts of land. In contrast, special structural requirements for rebuilding (such as elevated homes in flood-prone areas) are less likely to be deemed takings and thus be held compensable.

One legal question is whether the specific context of sea level rise due to climate change may offer the government defenses against regulatory takings claims not otherwise available. One possible starting point is *Lucas v. South Carolina Coastal Council*.[196] There, the Supreme Court dealt with a state beachfront management act aimed in large part at protecting the beach/dune system along the state's coast. Toward that end, the act sought to "discourage[e] new construction

---

[192] Fisher v. Town of Nags Head, 725 S.E.2d 99 (N.C. Ct. App.), *appeal denied*, 731 S.E.2d 166 (N.C. 2012).

[193] The opening paragraphs of this section draw their inspiration from *Coastal Retreat Measures*, *supra* note 149.

[194] Thus far, reactive retreat appears to be the more common, but the pattern may be shifting. For example, the Oregon Coastal Management Program has recommended "using land-use planning processes to address climate change." Oregon Coastal Management Program, Department of Land Conservation and Development, *Climate Ready Communities: A Strategy for Adapting to the Impacts of Climate Change on the Oregon Coast* at 5 (January 2009). *See generally* Anne Siders, MANAGED COASTAL RETREAT: A LEGAL HANDBOOK ON SHIFTING DEVELOPMENT AWAY FROM VULNERABLE AREAS (Columbia Law School Center for Climate Change Law, October, 2013).

[195] As the text notes, in contrast with regulatory prohibitions the mere removal of government development incentives is unlikely to be held a taking. *See, e.g.*, Texas Landowners Rights Ass'n v, Harris, 453 F. Supp. 1025 (D.D.C. 1978), *aff'd mem.*, 598 F.2d 311 (D.C. Cir. 1979), in connection with the National Flood Insurance Program. Another incentive-removing federal statute, the Coastal Barrier Resources Act, ended federal support (such as federal mortgage guarantees and federal flood insurance) for development on certain barrier islands. 16 U.S.C. §§ 3501-3510. It has generated no reported takings decisions.

[196] 505 U.S. 1003 (1992).

in close proximity to the beach/dune system and encourag[e] those who have erected structures too close to the system to retreat from it."[197] In particular, the plaintiff was barred from building any occupiable structure on his two beachfront lots. The Court pointedly rejected the state's assertion that the statute, by asserting avoidance of a public harm as its purpose, was immunized from takings liability. Only state action based on "background principles of the State's law of property and nuisance" was so protected,[198] said the Court, holding that the beachfront management act did not fall into that category. Traditional common law, it observed, rarely supports prohibiting the erection of a house.[199]

Lucas suggests that the possibility that a tract of land will be submerged in the future as the result of climate change may not be sufficient to deflect takings or other legal challenges against a development prohibition on that tract—at least when, as in *Lucas*, the prohibition eliminates all land value. In *Lucas*, not even the fact that plaintiff's lots had been submerged at various times in the previous 40 years was enough to shield the state from takings liability. And while public trust doctrine has been held to be a "background principle" immunizing the state,[200] there is no support for any extension of public trust doctrine, as a defense to takings claims, to lands not below the mean high water mark when the development prohibition is imposed. Arguably, however, the question remains open.[201]

The *Lucas* decision, rendered in 1992, did not consider climate change. And because *Lucas* dealt with a "total taking"—that is, a regulatory restriction eliminating *all* use and value in a tract of land—it did not deal with takings law factors confined to *less-than-total* elimination of use and value. One such factor is the extent to which the government action interfered with the landowner's "reasonable investment-backed expectations" (RIBEs). The RIBEs question here revolves around recent or future purchasers of land prone to climate-change-induced extreme weather, such as flooding. Can such purchasers be charged with constructive knowledge of the scientific consensus that climate change will bring about more frequent instances of extreme weather in the future? Can such purchasers, as a result, be held "on notice" that state or local governments might restrict development of such parcels in the future, weakening any claim that such restrictions interfere with *reasonable* expectations of development when the land was acquired? Would the existence of a widely publicized government retreat proposal at the time when the land was acquired strengthen an on-notice/absence-of-RIBEs argument by the government? And could states bolster this defense by requiring that all purchasers of disaster-prone land be given written notice prior to purchase of the risks to which they were exposing themselves?[202] Even today, "[s]everal [state] disclosure statutes require inclusion of whether the

---

[197] *Id.* at 1021 n.10.

[198] *Id.* at 1029.

[199] *Id.* at 1031.

[200] *See, e.g.*, McQueen v. South Carolina Coastal Council, 580 S.E.2d 116, 119 n.5 (S.C. 2003).

[201] *See* F. Patrick Hubbard, *The Impact of Lucas on Coastal Development: Background Principles, the Public Trust Doctrine and Global Warming*, 16 Southeastern Envtl. L. J. 65, 80 (2007).

[202] One commentator would answer yes to both the footnoted text question, involving written notice, and the immediately preceding text questions, involving only constructive knowledge. He argues that "increasing awareness of [sea level rise] and its impacts as well as distribution of such information should inform analysis of coastal owners' RIBE in legal claims that government regulation or action has taken private property." Thomas Ruppert, *Reasonable Investment-Backed Expectations: Should Notice of Rising Seas Lead to Falling Expectations for Coastal Property Purchasers?*, 26 J. Land Use & Envtl. L. 239 (2011). Proposals to require landowners in designated areas to inform buyers of potential sea level rise are being considered in several states.

property has been affected by floods or is in a flood zone or plain."[203] The extremely thin case law on whether such notice undercuts a taking claim based on development restrictions points to notice not making much difference.[204] But it is far too early to regard the matter as settled.

One commentator has raised the argument that coastal states would be in a better position to defend takings claims if they cast managed-retreat land use regulation as public health measures, based on the effects of sea level rise and more severe coastal storms.[205] Such public health effects might result from salt-water intrusion into drinking water supplies, power outages, and stormwaters contaminated by overflowed refineries and chemical plants, dry cleaners, service stations, flooded vehicles, and sewage. Takings law has traditionally resisted finding takings based on governmental public health measures.

The question has also been raised whether local jurisdictions might be successfully sued in the opposite situation—that is, where they *fail* to restrict development despite having knowledge that flooding may occur, following which the permitted development is damaged by flooding or exacerbates flooding on other properties.[206]

Further inland, the National Flood Insurance Program (NFIP) becomes a central player in discouraging construction in flood-prone areas[207]—floods that in some instances may become more severe or frequent as the result of climate change-related sea level rise or extreme rainfall. A local jurisdiction's participation in the NFIP is voluntary. It is embodied in an agreement under which the community adopts floodplain management ordinances meeting minimum NFIP requirements for regulating new-construction design in "special flood hazard areas,"[208] and use restrictions in the regulatory floodway. In return, the federal government makes subsidized federal flood insurance available to landowners in those jurisdictions.

Courts have unanimously rejected takings suits based on NFIP-inspired floodplain ordinances, or similar non-NFIP floodplain ordinances.[209] Should future sea level rise lead to stricter federal conditions for flood insurance in the form of stricter floodplain ordinances, takings issues inevitably will rear their head once more. A recent change in the law, directing the NFIP to consider future sea level rise and not just historical flood data in creating floodplain maps, could provide additional basis for such stricter requirements.[210] One can expect, however, that the

---

[203] *Id.* at 260, citing as an example Cal. Civ. Code § 1103(v)(1)(A).

[204] *Id.* at 266-267.

[205] Robin K. Craig, *Of Sea Level Rise and Superstorms: The Public Health Police Power as a Means of Defending Against "Takings" Challenges to Coastal Regulation*, course materials submitted at the 16th Annual Conference on Litigating Takings Challenges to Land Use and Environmental Regulations (NYU School of Law Nov. 22, 2013) (on file with author).

[206] *See generally* James Wilkins, *Is Sea Level Rise "Foreseeable"? Does It Matter?*, 26 Vt. J. Envtl L. 437 (2011).

[207] 42 U.S.C. §§ 4001-4128.

[208] Special flood hazard areas are mapped by the Federal Emergency Management Agency, which administers the NFIP generally. 44 C.F.R. § 59.2(b).

[209] *See, e.g.,* Adolph v. Federal Emergency Management Agency, 854 F.2d 732 (5th Cir. 1988); Gove v. Zoning Bd. Of Appeals, 831 N.E.2d 865, 871-875 (Mass. 2005); Responsible Citizens in Opposition to Floodplain Ordinance v. City of Asheville, 302 S.E.2d 204 (N.C. 1983). *But see* McDougal v. County of Imperial, 942 F.2d 668 (9th Cir. 1991) (fact that government's purpose in floodway designation was legitimate does not automatically preclude regulatory takings claim).

[210] P.L. 112-141, Div. F, tit. II, subtit. A (Biggert-Waters Flood Insurance Reform Act of 2012) §§ 100215(d)(1), 100216(b)(3)(D).

---

current judicial refusal to impute to the United States any takings liability for such local ordinances will continue to stand as long as their adoption remains voluntary.[211]

Finally, local jurisdictions have asked whether their potential disinvestment in public infrastructure in low-lying areas (such as armoring, roads and bridges, and wastewater treatment plants) might raise takings issues.[212] The aim of such disinvestment would be to hold down repair and restoration costs as the result of floods and sea level rise, and to discourage new development in such areas or promote removal of existing development. Affected property owners, however, may not be so civic-minded. For example, a state's decision to discontinue maintenance of a shoreside road that is eroding away might lead those dependent on that road for access to their land to assert a taking by denial of access.[213] The viability of such takings claims will vary widely with the facts. No reported takings decisions at all exist in response to the federal government's disinvestment in the development of coastal barrier islands through the Coastal Barrier Resources Act.[214] On the other hand, disinvestment in public infrastructure may be dicier if the courts perceive a state or local government duty to maintain existing infrastructure.[215] Presumably, takings problems can be lessened by announcing disinvestment many years (even a decade or more) in advance; such "amortization periods" have been effective in other factual contexts, such as billboard removal programs, in deflecting takings claims.[216] Governments might also take care not to allow disinvestment in an area to get too far ahead of the retreat activity of those living and working there.

---

[211] *Adolph*, 854 F.2d 732 (holding that Federal Emergency Management Agency cannot be sued for taking based on parish's adoption of floodplain regulations to qualify for NFIP, because adoption was not federally coerced).

[212] This paragraph discussing disinvestment in public infrastructure was inspired by David Lewis, *Constitutional Property Law Analysis of State and Local Government Disinvestment in Infrastructure as a Coastal Adaptation Strategy* (2012) (student paper on file with author). *See also* Travis M. Brennan, *Redefining the American Coastline: Can the Government Withdraw Basic Services From the Coast and Avoid Takings Claims?*, 14 Ocean & Coastal L. J. 101 (2008).

[213] *See, e.g.*, Jordan v. St. Johns County, 63 So. 3d 835 (Fla. App.), *rev. denied*, 77 So. 3d 647 (Fla. 2011); Jordan v. Canton, 265 A.2d 96 (Me. 1970).

[214] 16 U.S.C. §§ 3501-3510.

[215] *See, e.g.*, *St. Johns County*, 63 So. 3d 835 (argument that county has so failed in its duty to maintain road as to deprive property owner of access states taking claim; government inaction in the face of an affirmative duty to act can support taking claim). *Compare* Bailey v. Preserve Rural Roads of Madison County, Inc., 394 S.W.3d 350 (Ky. 2011) (noting that if a road closing deprives an owner of reasonable access to his land, "he is entitled to damages," but nonetheless finding no authority that county's refusal to maintain road in good repair is an unconstitutional infringement of a landowner's right of access). *See generally* William B. Stoebuck, *The Property Right of Access Versus the Power of Eminent Domain*, 47 Texas L. Rev. 733 (1969).

[216] "Amortization programs dovetail nicely with the traditional notion of land-use planning that nonconforming uses should be phased out gradually rather than terminated immediately." R. Meltz, D.H. Merriam, and R.M. Frank, THE TAKINGS ISSUE 433 (Island Press 1999). The value of an amortization period for avoiding takings is well-established. *See, e.g.*, Naegele Outdoor Advertising Co. v. City of Durham, 844 F.2d 172, 177 (4th Cir. 1988).

VII. Responding To and Rebuilding After Natural Disasters

A. Responding

Legal questions inevitably arise as to whether public and private actions taken in an emergency, climate-change-related or otherwise, are subject to the same legal requirements as when there is no emergency. And, for that matter, what constitutes an emergency—a term generally left undefined in statutes. There is no explicit, across-the-board exemption in any federal environmental statute for emergency response.

A sampler of less-than-across-the-board statutory provisions reflecting the need for relaxed regulation in emergencies might include, first, the Clean Air Act. Under this act, EPA "may temporarily waive a control or prohibition respecting the use of a fuel or fuel additive" where "extreme and unusual" fuel supply circumstances exist as the result of a "natural disaster" not reasonably foreseeable.[217] Under the Comprehensive Environmental Response, Compensation, and Liability Act (CERCLA), government emergency response to releases or threatened releases of hazardous substances ("removal actions"), as when a flood jeopardizes containment of hazardous chemicals at a site, can be done with less prior study and investigation than is required for permanent cleanups ("remedial actions").[218] And Council on Environmental Quality regulations implementing the National Environmental Policy Act (NEPA) say that where emergency circumstances require a federal agency to take action without observing the regulations, the agency should consult with the Council about "alternative arrangements."[219] Federal actions not needed to control the immediate impacts of the emergency, however, remain fully subject to NEPA review.

In addition to the above statutory provisions, federal agencies have invoked their inherent enforcement discretion to issue assurances that due to special circumstances, a regulatory requirement will not be enforced for a brief period in the affected area.[220]

B. Rebuilding

Following a natural calamity in which structures are destroyed, several legal questions may arise as to rebuilding (or substantially repairing). The first is whether there are restrictions or outright prohibitions on rebuilding dictated by a desire to minimize damage in the future. Such adaptation

---

[217] Clean Air Act § 211(c)(4)(C)(ii); 42 U.S.C. § 7545(c)(4)(C)(ii). EPA has issued such fuel waivers frequently, as after Hurricanes Katrina and Sandy. *See* http://epa.gov/enforcement/air/fuel-waivers.html.

[218] CERCLA § 101(23), 42 U.S.C. § 9601(23) (definition of "removal"); CERCLA § 101(24), 42 U.S.C. § 9601(24) (definition of "removal action").

[219] 40 C.F.R. § 1506.11. See also the NEPA regulations of the Corps of Engineers, which call on that agency, in responding to emergencies, to refer actions with potentially significant environmental impacts to the CEQ as to NEPA arrangements "[w]hen possible." 33 C.F.R. § 230.8.

[220] Invoking this enforcement discretion after Hurricane Sandy, for example, EPA issued a No Action Assurance letter saying that from November 2 to 17, 2012, it would not pursue violations of Clean Air Act vapor recovery requirements for fuel loading and unloading at certain facilities in Massachusetts, Maryland, New Jersey, and New York. Available at http://epa.gov/enforcement/air/documents/policies/mobile/naa-vaporrecoverymamd110512.pdf.

concerns were treated in Section VI.B. Another question, our topic here, is whether the rebuilding of a structure essentially as it was before, in the very same location, is subject to the full range of environmental requirements applicable if the structure were being built there for the first time. Here, besides the question of what constitutes an emergency, there is the added issue whether the replacement structure is essentially the same as its predecessor (changes are always made to some degree). As with responding to emergencies (previous section), there appears to be no explicit, across-the-board exemption in federal environmental law.

Probably the broadest exemption in federal statutes for rebuilding structures is that in the Stafford Disaster Relief Act. The act decrees that no environmental impact statement (EIS) under NEPA is required for "[a]n action which is taken or assistance which is provided pursuant to [the Act], which has the effect of restoring a facility substantially to its condition prior to the disaster or emergency."[221] Also as to NEPA, Department of Transportation regulations allow for categorical exclusions from EIS preparation for reconstruction (whether prompted by a disaster or not) of highways, bridges, and rail and bus facilities.[222] Limited NEPA case law on the replacement issue indicates that federal involvement in the construction of an essentially similar replacement facility does not require an EIS—as long as the environment *with* the original facility is accepted as the status quo baseline.[223] This qualifier suggests that the passage of several years before the new facility is built, accompanied by a change in the environment at the site, might cause the *changed* environment to be viewed as the baseline. With the changed environment as the baseline, the federal action might be seen as having significant impact, triggering the EIS requirement.

Outside of NEPA, the Clean Water Act affords an exemption from its requirement of permits for the discharge of dredged or fill material "for the purpose of emergency reconstruction ... of currently serviceable structures such as dikes, dams, levees, ... and transportation structures."[224] Also, three nationwide permits issued by the Corps of Engineers under this permit program cover reconstruction in varying degrees, relieving the applicant of the more expensive and time-consuming process of applying for an individual permit.[225]

Other questions arise when localities seek to use federal disaster relief funds to rebuild more resiliently than before. Following Hurricane Irene, for example, Vermont asked FEMA for reimbursement under the Stafford Act for upgraded culverts designed to handle more water. The problem was not their larger-than-before size, since FEMA regulations allow funding of replacement facilities different from the pre-existing design if the applicable codes when the disaster strikes dictate a change in facility design.[226] Reportedly, however, FEMA initially denied reimbursement on the ground that the state's standards for rebuilding culverts gave the state

---

[221] 42 U.S.C. § 5159.

[222] 23 C.F.R. § 771.117(d).

[223] Sierra Club v. Hassell, 636 F.2d 1095, 1099 (5ᵗʰ Cir. 1981) (replacement of bridge destroyed by hurricane requires no EIS). *Accord,* Citizens for the Scenic Severn River Bridge, Inc. v. Skinner, 802 F. Supp. 1325, 1333 (D. Md. 1991).

[224] 33 U.S.C. § 1344(f)(1)(B).

[225] *See* Nationwide Permit No. 3 (repair, rehabilitation, or replacement of any previously authorized, currently serviceable structure), No. 31 (maintenance of existing flood control facilities), and No. 45 (restoration of upland areas damaged by storms, floods, or other discrete events, including bank stabilization). 77 Fed. Reg. 10,270 (February 21, 2012).

[226] 40 C.F.R. § 206.226(d)(1)-(5).

enough discretion that FEMA was not assured the standards met its requirement that they apply "uniformly to all similar types of facilities.... "[227]

VIII. Immigration and Refugee Law[228]

United Nations High Commissioner for Refugees Antonio Guterres has said: "Climate change is today one of the main drivers of forced displacement, both directly through impact on environment—not allowing people to live any more in the areas where they were traditionally living—and as a trigger of extreme poverty and conflict."[229] Climate-related migrants, however, are not considered a "protected class" of people in international law or U.S. immigration law, nor is there a specific legal framework or entity responsible for their displacement.

In international law, the foundational document is the 1951 Convention Relating to the Status of Refugees, which defines "refugee" as a person who "owing to a well-founded fear of being persecuted for reasons of race, religion, nationality, membership of a particular social group, or political opinion, is outside the country of his nationality."[230] This definition is unlikely to embrace climate change refugees since they do not suffer "persecution," and certainly not for the stated reasons.[231] In addition, it is widely held that for the foreseeable future, most people displaced by climate change will stay within their own countries, and thus fall outside the definition of refugee because not "outside the country of [their] nationality."[232]

Similarly, the United States has long held to the principle that it will not return a foreign national to a country where his life or freedom would be threatened, but this principle does not encompass economic or environmental migrants. The Immigration and Nationality Act (INA) requires foreign nationals seeking asylum or refugee status to demonstrate a well-founded fear that, if returned home, they will be persecuted based upon the five characteristics listed in the Convention (above).[233] Provisions also exist in the INA to offer temporary protected status or

---

[227] 40 C.F.R. § 206.226(d)(4). *See* Justin B. Clancy and Jessica Grannis, *Lessons Learned from Irene: Climate Change, Federal Disaster Relief, and Barriers to Adaptive Reconstruction* (Georgetown Climate Center December 2013).

[228] This section of the report was written by Ruth Ellen Wasem, Specialist in Immigration Policy, CRS Domestic Social Policy Division. *See generally* Jane McAdam, CLIMATE CHANGE, FORCED MIGRATION, AND INTERNATIONAL LAW (2012); Etienne Piguet et al. (eds.), MIGRATION AND CLIMATE CHANGE (2011).

[229] "Conflicts Fuelled by Climate Change Causing New Refugee Crisis, Warns UN," by Julian Borger, *The Guardian*, (June 17, 2008), available online at http://www.guardian.co.uk/environment/2008/jun/17/climatechange.food. See *also* United Nations High Commissioner on Refugees, THE STATE OF THE WORLD'S REFUGEES 2012: IN SEARCH OF SOLIDARITY ch. 7 ("Displacement, Climate Change, and Natural Disasters"), summary available at http://www.unhcr.org/publications/unhcr/sowr2012.

[230] The United States is not a party to the 1951 Convention but is a party to the 1967 Protocol Relating to the Status of Refugees, which amends the Convention. 19 U.S. Treaties 6223.

[231] *See, e.g.*, CLIMATE CHANGE, FORCED MIGRATION, AND INTERNATIONAL LAW, *supra* note 228, at 42-48 (2012). The text view—non-inclusion of those displaced by climate change as "refugees"—is the view of the vast majority of observers. Recently reported is a New Zealand court's rejection of an argument by a Kirabatian man that he should not be deported after his visa expired because climate change was making his home country uninhabitable. The court, again reportedly, found no evidence that the man would be "persecuted" within the meaning of the 1951 convention. Sean McLemon, *Climate Refugees Could Catch World's Courts Off Guard* (Law 360 December 16, 2013). Going against the prevailing view, however, is Jessica B. Cooper, *Environmental Refugees: Meeting the Requirements of the Refugee Definition*, 6 N.Y.U. Envtl. L. J. 480, 501-528 (1998).

[232] MIGRATION AND CLIMATE CHANGE, *supra* note 228, at 289.

[233] See definition of "refugee" in INA section 101(a)(42); 8 U.S.C. § 1101(a)(42). This definition governs the reach of (continued...)

---

relief from removal when natural disasters occur or when violence and civil unrest erupt in spots around the world. While temporary protected status may benefit people stranded in the United States because of natural disasters, it is only short-term relief from removal.[234]

Author Contact Information

Robert Meltz
Legislative Attorney
rmeltz@crs.loc.gov, 7-7891

(...continued)

INA section 207, 8 U.S.C. § 1157, governing admissions based on humanitarian concerns, and INA section 208, 8 U.S.C. § 1158, governing asylum.

[234] For further background, see CRS Report RL31269, *Refugee Admissions and Resettlement Policy*, by Andorra Bruno; CRS Report R41753, *Asylum and "Credible Fear" Issues in U.S. Immigration Policy*, by Ruth Ellen Wasem; and CRS Report RS20844, *Temporary Protected Status: Current Immigration Policy and Issues*, by Ruth Ellen Wasem and Karma Ester.